LAND OF OPPORTUNITY

ALSO BY THE AUTHOR

FAT CITY: *How Washington Wastes Your Taxes*
WASHINGTON — CITY OF SCANDALS

LAND OF OPPORTUNITY

ALSO BY THE AUTHOR

FAT CITY: *How Washington Wastes Your Taxes*

WASHINGTON — CITY OF SCANDALS

LAND OF OPPORTUNITY

THE ENTREPRENEURIAL SPIRIT IN AMERICA

by Donald Lambro

LITTLE, BROWN AND COMPANY

BOSTON TORONTO

FIRST EDITION

Library of Congress Cataloging-in-Publication Data

Lambro, Donald.
Land of opportunity.

Includes index.
1. Economic forecasting—United States. 2. United States—Economic conditions—1981– . 3. United States—Economic policy—1981– . 4. Entrepreneur. 5. Supply-side economics—United States. I. Title.
HC106.8.L34 1986 338.973 86-10566
ISBN 0-316-51289-3

MV

Published simultaneously in Canada
by Little, Brown & Company (Canada) Limited

PRINTED IN THE UNITED STATES OF AMERICA

To my wife, Jackie

If you have built castles in the air, your work need not be lost; that is where they should be. Now put the foundations under them. All men want, not something to do *with*, but something to do, or rather something to *be*.

— Henry David Thoreau
Walden

Contents

Acknowledgments

I AM DEEPLY INDEBTED to a number of people who helped me tell the story of economic growth in the 1980s.

First and foremost, I am very grateful to writer M. Stanton Evans and his National Journalism Center, a Capitol Hill organization that brings talented young journalists to Washington to get a taste of working with the national news media. I was fortunate to receive the benefit of several of the center's brightest and most promising interns, who assisted me with some of the research for this book.

My special thanks to Joy Anthony, an immensely talented economics writer who one day may be the next Sylvia Porter, for her untiring and always cheerful assistance.

I am also grateful for the prodigious help of interns Jeffrey Tucker, an economics graduate from Howard Paine University; William Ziener, a Grove City College political science graduate; David Maxson, an economics major at California's Claremont College; and Michael Fumento, a University of Illinois law graduate.

My thanks also to Dr. Richard Rahn, chief economist for the U.S. Chamber of Commerce, for his typically perceptive insights; writer and editor Richard Vigilante, for his always valuable counsel; Mac Carey, administrative assistant to Congressman Jim Courter of New Jersey, for his special assistance; Roberta Miller, my agent at United Media, for her encouragement and savvy advice; Ray Roberts, senior editor at Little, Brown and Company, for his patience, understanding, and steadfast support; senior editor Sharon Nelton of *Nation's Business* magazine for her very helpful ideas; Amy Bayer for her additional research assistance; John E. Bregger, chief of the Employment and Unemployment Analysis Division in the U.S. Bureau of Labor Statistics; Richard M. Devens, Jr., economist for the U.S. Bureau of Labor Statistics; William Orzechowski, director of federal budget policy for the U.S. Chamber of Commerce; and journalist Don Caldwell for his meticulous reading of the manuscript. Finally, a special thank you to all the entrepreneurs who took time from their busy schedules to talk about their enterprises and their inspiring dreams for the future.

Introduction

THERE IS MORE of my past in this book than I fully realized when I was writing it. My father emigrated from Albania to America as a young boy during the early 1920s, sent here by his widowed mother in the hope that he would find a brighter future than the poor life that faced him in post–World War I Eastern Europe. He had heard much of America and its promise of wealth and opportunity, and as young as he was, he wanted desperately to come here to make his way in the world. Carrying a small bag of belongings, with his boat and train fare carefully sewn into the lining of his native clothes by his mother, he set out alone on a long and perilous journey to the New World in July 1923 at the tender age of thirteen. Starting out on foot past fields of wheat, he made his way, with the help of people his mother had painstakingly arranged to escort him along portions of his journey, to Greece, then across the Adriatic Sea by a small boat to Italy, and then by train to Naples, where he boarded a steamer bound for America and the port of immigrants, New York's Ellis Island.

Somehow, often with the help of perfect strangers, he managed to find his way through the confusion of immigration officials and inspectors and board a train to Massachusetts, where an uncle in Fitchburg had agreed to take him in. The son of a hardworking stonemason and builder, my father would eventually learn a trade as a barber and beautician, marry another Albanian immigrant who had settled in Worcester, Massachusetts, and open up his own barbershop in an affluent Boston suburb. He worked hard, holding two jobs during World War II, and eventually expanded his business, providing employment to other barbers. He saved and invested his money wisely, bought property, built his own home and, with the help of my mother, an industrious and frugal woman, raised three children. For my father and mother, America kept its enduring promise as the land of opportunity, and their story is the essence of America, told and retold from generation to generation of immigrants and their offspring who have made America the great nation it has become. My parents' belief in hard work and in their endlessly repeated plea to "make something of yourself" has profoundly shaped my life and my beliefs in the work ethic and American enterprise. Their recognition and appreciation of everything America has given them is very much woven into the fabric of this book and the story it seeks to tell once more.

America, I believe, has entered the Age of the Entrepreneur and a new era of enterprise, capitalist expansion, and growth. The abundant evidence for this is all about us, but one stunning fact alone reveals what is happening in today's resilient economy: a seemingly inexhaustible supply of entrepreneurs is establishing a record number of new businesses each year — more than 2.5 million companies since 1980 — creating millions of new jobs and career opportunities for all Americans. *Inc.*, a monthly magazine, bullishly dedicated to chronicling the entrepreneurial spirit that has reignited the U.S. economy, observes that "many of the big Fortune 500 companies have been laying people off while the dynamic young growth companies have been hiring, expanding and purchasing like there's no tomorrow. The Entrepreneurial Revolution is on."

I further believe that because of this new era of enterprise, the promise of America — that every American is free to climb as high as his or her talents and ambition and vision of the future will allow — is more alive and more accessible today than at any other time in our history. In an attempt to demonstrate this, I have assembled a number of stories from entrepreneurs of all walks of life, rich and poor, young and old, who have toiled and taken risks and built enterprises that provided new jobs, higher incomes, and expanding opportunities for their fellow citizens. It is this sector of our economy that is conducting the only truly effective war against poverty.

At its core *Land of Opportunity* is an examination of what has occurred in the economy in the 1970s and 1980s to make the American dream a greater reality: the social, political, attitudinal, educational, and legislative changes that have put America back on the road toward increasing economic growth. These changes have had a profoundly important effect on the economic course America is now pursuing, even though they have received surprisingly little attention and analysis from the anchormen and pundits of the national news media and the academicians within our major institutions of higher learning.

For example, Ronald Reagan's three-year tax cuts begun in 1981, which were preceded by a bipartisan move in the late 1970s — initially opposed by President Jimmy Carter — to cut the capital gains tax rate in order to spur capital investment, have not only had an enormous effect on stimulating economic growth, new business formation, and job creation, they have changed basic public perceptions on fundamental economic issues.

The significant degree to which America's economic and political attitudes have been altered was strikingly apparent when President Reagan, cementing his mandate for leadership with a forty-nine-state landslide reelection in 1984, offered his tax reform proposal for "fairness, growth, and simplicity" in 1985. His plan proposed reducing the maximum federal income tax rate to 35 percent. Ironically, Reagan's radical tax reform proposal had more opposition from the political right, which wanted to bring the maximum tax rate down to 30 or 25 percent. Even the Democratic Bradley-Gephardt tax reform proposal sought a maximum tax rate of 30 percent. It was a sign of the changing times that few if any politicians or political groups were demanding that the top individual tax rates should be raised, even though as little as five years earlier many people had still been arguing for, or at least supporting the maintenance of the top federal tax rate, which was 70 percent. "Clearly," says Dr. Richard Rahn, chief economist for the U.S. Chamber of Commerce, "there has been a fundamental shift in American attitudes. People are now concerned about economic growth. Economic growth has become the nation's priority."

Land of Opportunity surveys many other economic, political, and attitudinal changes that have taken place in an attempt not only to put into sharper perspective what is happening economically in America today, but also to chart the future economic direction in which America and much of the world will be moving.

Yet for too many Americans, the economic recovery and the American dream remain distant and unreachable. Drawing these Americans and their communities into the economic mainstream is one of the chief challenges for future economic growth initiatives. This is why much of this book is devoted to examining the numerous bureaucratic and policy obstacles to greater economic growth — largely erected by government — that still remain stubbornly in place. The productive and creative potential of America's entrepreneurial capabilities will not reach urban and rural pockets of poverty until these barriers to growth are dismantled.

I believe that the expansion of economic growth, both here and abroad, will be the pivotal political and social issue for the remainder of this decade and beyond. How to bring about greater levels of growth and increased prosperity for all is the purpose of *Land of Opportunity*. It is meant to remind us that healthy, robust economic growth — providing full employment without inflation — can only be achieved through the freest possible economic system, with the lowest possible tax rate on profit. This is the emerging economic and political consensus that is sweeping America in the decade of the 1980s, a consensus that promises to lift our nation to new levels of achievement and greatness. This book is both a reaffirmation of these axioms and a celebration of the entrepreneurial spirit they nourish.

Donald Lambro
WASHINGTON, D.C.

LAND
OF
OPPORTUNITY

The erosion of our confidence in the future is threatening to destroy the social and the political fabric of America.

— *President Jimmy Carter*, 1979

The economic ills we suffer . . . will not go away in days, weeks, or months, but they will go away. They will go away because we as Americans have the capacity now, as we've had in the past, to do whatever needs to be done to preserve this last and greatest bastion of freedom.

— *President Ronald Reagan*, 1981

CHAPTER I

The Era of Enterprise

"IT WAS THE BEST of times, it was the worst of times." If ever this famous paradoxical line by Charles Dickens aptly described a recent period in American history, it surely was the beginning of the 1980s, when the nation had begun its descent into the worst recession in more than forty years.

Just a year before, President Jimmy Carter appeared on nationwide television to tell Americans that they were suffering from "a crisis of confidence," saying in essence that the country was in the grip of what a top Carter adviser called a "national malaise." It was a period, too, when the poverty rate was worsening significantly after years of improvement; when the nation had been threatened with severe energy shortages and government experts were warning that the world was rapidly running out of oil, among other natural resources; when America's aging smokestack factories were closing with increasing frequency; when polls showed many Americans had little if any confidence in their country's economic future; and when punishing double-digit interest and inflation rates were pounding the economy to its knees.

But it was also a time when new business formations were climbing to record highs, when America's high-technology enterprises were bursting with invention and innovation and the promise of greater prosperity; when visionary risk takers were coming out of the woodwork of the economy to form small to mid-sized businesses that offered new hope and opportunities for Americans; when the entrepreneur was becoming the new American folk hero and the fresh young faces of business pioneers like Steven Jobs, the developer of the personal computer and the founder of Apple Computer, Inc., were gracing the cover of *Time* and other national magazines as if they were movie stars.

Yet, strangely, during this paradoxical period only the dark side of the economy was being examined and emphasized by America's merchants of doom in the national news media. A *Wall Street Journal* survey of the television networks' nightly news coverage of the economy during the first six months of 1983 noted that 95 percent of the monthly economic reports issued by the government showed positive signs about the nation's economic growth. But the *Journal* discovered that out of the 104 news stories the networks did on these reports, 86 percent painted a largely negative view of the economy. The survey further found that as the economy continued to rebound in the last six months of 1983, the networks still portrayed America as largely being in a recession.

Indeed, throughout the darkest days of the 1981–82 recession, I especially remember CBS News anchorman Dan Rather regularly reporting the number of business bankruptcies that were then occurring throughout the economy with growing frequency. The news cameras were there to record the closure of rundown factories, the anguish of laid-off workers, and the bitterness of business managers forced to close their doors forever. The bankruptcy statistics gave further proof, if any was needed, that the United States was experiencing its worst recession since the Great Depression. It was far easier, it seemed, to record a tire plant closing in Akron, Ohio, or report the grim aggregate figures from the Bureau of Labor Statistics than it was to tell the story of the opening of a chain of new computer stores or fast-food franchises and project its broader ramifications for the economy.

Dan Rather and his colleagues elsewhere in the national news media neglected to report another vital statistic and in the process not only gave Americans a terribly distorted picture of what was happening to the economy but offered little if any reason to hope that the situation could and would get better. Significantly, they failed in virtually every instance to report the number of business formations that were occurring simultaneously throughout the country.

Surprisingly, even during the depths of the recession, the economy was still giving birth to nearly 600,000 new business enterprises a year — 80 percent more than the economy was creating in 1975. True, thousands of businesses were dying, but thousands of new enterprises were appearing to take their place. In fact, many more were being born than were dying. Something exciting and confident, and even courageous, was emerging on America's Main Street. It was the indomitable spirit of American enterprise, eager to seek and make its fortune and in the process bring new jobs, hope, and opportunity to millions of Americans.

Unfortunately, Americans during this period were shown only "the worst of times" by most of the national news media, which selectively chose to report only one set of statistics, as if to prove that President Ronald Reagan's critics were right when they predicted during Reagan's 1980 campaign that his tax- and budget-cutting prescriptions would plunge the economy into a deep and long-lasting recession. In fact, the national news media's propensity to dish out only the business failure rate was tantamount to reporting the number of persons who die each year, bemoaning the death rate's attritional effect on the population, while ignoring the number of births.

In point of fact, the steadily increasing birth rate in new businesses has not only been impressive, it has been the envy of the world. In 1980, the year before Reagan assumed office, the number of new business formations reached 533,520 — an increase of 8,955 over the previous year. This, in spite of the fact that the inflation rate was a withering 13.5 percent for the year; the prime rate, that is, the interest rate that banks charge their best customers, had reached an insufferable 15.3 percent; the Federal Reserve Board was mercilessly squeezing the money supply in a frantic effort to deflate the economy; and mounting government regulation of the economy had reached the suffocating point where the U.S. Department of Labor was threatening legal action against a group of women in the Green Mountains of Vermont after federal agents learned that they were knitting winter outerwear in their homes for profit, which was forbidden by an obscure federal regulation. It would have been appropriate to ask that if the economy could produce a modest increase in the number of businesses in such a hostile economic climate, what could it do in an environment of tax cut incentives, lower inflation, and less government regulation?

By 1981, while President Reagan was valiantly pushing his spending restraints and supply-side tax cuts through Congress, and while much of the economy continued to deteriorate, the number of new businesses still zoomed upward to 581,242, a remarkable 8.9 percent jump over 1980. Notably, this growth rate in new enterprises occurred at a time when the prime lending rate had reached nearly 19 percent for the year and the flames of inflation, though somewhat lower, were still searing the economy at levels of 10.4 percent.

As the Federal Reserve Board continued to apply the brakes to the economy in 1982, the recession deepened. The prime rate was slightly lower but still at a punishing 14.8 percent. Yet the economy still gave birth to 566,942 new businesses that year. Though down by 2.4 percent as a result of the crushing recession, this was nevertheless a remarkable testament to the tenacity, resilience, and resourcefulness of American enterprise that beat within the heart of the economy. Overall, the economy had still produced a 6.2 percent increase in business formations during 1981 and 1982, the two worst years of the recession.

Nonetheless, throughout this period the oracles in the Washington news media's Temple of Doom chose to emphasize only the failure rate for *all* businesses — not just new ones — which was 61.3 percent. What no one bothered to mention was that this failure rate was actually lower than in 1964, when a 64.4 percent bankruptcy rate scourged U.S. businesses. Yet the economy was considered perfectly healthy at the time, with only a 0.7 percent inflation rate and a jobless level of 6.4 percent. Wages and hourly earnings were at an all-time high in 1964, productivity of individual workers was at its highest rate since 1955, and the prime rate was relatively constant at 4.5 percent. Clearly, the business failure rates can be high even when the economy is healthy.

In truth, what the business failure rate demonstrates, among other things, is increased business speculation. It is in its truest sense the product of an optimistic view of the economy's future. Obviously, any speculative activity in a market economy carries with it the possibility of failure. And the more speculation by entrepreneurs, the higher the number of failures.

But the failure rate also is an expression of fierce competition at work, coldly weeding out the efficient from the inefficient, the productive from the unproductive, the innovative from the unimaginative. Perhaps not every business folded because it deserved to, but the cold, objective, and highly competitive marketplace was doing its job. "The success of the economy depends on competition," said the President's Council of Economic Advisers in its 1983 annual report. "Competition requires that firms adapt to changing market demands and calls upon them to adjust to fluctuating capital market conditions. Competition breaks down entrenched market positions, unsettles comfortable managerial lives and provides incentives for innovative forms of business organization and finance. In sum, competition plays a central role in the evolution of the economy; it promotes efficient modes of production and eliminates processes and organizational structures that have outlived their usefulness."

Spurred by increased capital investment and risk taking, which was largely a direct result of the 1981 tax cuts and business investment incentives, 1983 proved to be another vintage year for business formations. The economy produced a total of 600,400 new enterprises that year. The number of new businesses shot up again in 1984, to an all-time high of 634,991, a stunning 19 percent increase over 1980. By comparison, the business formation rate during President Lyndon Johnson's 1965–68 term of office, which LBJ anointed as the Great Society, totaled an anemic 8.9 percent.

Significant increases in gross domestic investment provided further evidence that the tax cuts had spurred businesses to invest and expand and had encouraged entrepreneurs to open new enterprises. From 1981 to 1984, gross domestic investment increased 38.9 percent, compared to only 13 percent during Jimmy Carter's four years, when the economy was burdened with higher marginal tax rates and growing inflation. By further comparison, gross domestic investment actually declined by 5 percent between 1972 and 1976, during the Richard Nixon–Gerald Ford presidencies. These figures are adjusted for inflation, in constant 1972 dollars.

Between 1981 and 1984, investment growth saw its largest increases in any four-year period in four decades. In 1981 alone, even as the economy slid further into the recession, there was a 10.7 percent increase in investment, attributable in part to a new, positive view of the future of the economy that was slowly developing in the business community. But the largest rise in gross domestic investment occurred between 1982 and 1984 — increasing by 54.5 percent from the third quarter of 1982 to the third quarter of 1984. The largest comparable increase during the Carter years was 28.3 percent.

The spectacular recovery of 1983 and 1984 was dramatically reflected in the real Gross National Product (GNP), which robustly grew at an average annual rate of 6 percent during this period.

Inflation, which had been raging at 10.4 percent in 1981, fell to a toothless 3.2 percent by 1983.

Interest rates, which had reached 21 percent in 1980, fell by more than 50 percent by 1984. By the end of 1985, the prime rate was hovering around 10 percent, and interest rates for conventional home mortgages were averaging about 11 percent.

The nation's median family income was also steadily rising by a healthy 3.3 percent in 1984 (to $26,433), the fastest rate of increase since 1972.

Meanwhile, unemployment, always a lagging economic indicator in any recovery, fell from an annual rate of nearly 10 percent for 1982 to 7.1 percent by the end of 1985, the lowest unemployment level in more than five years. At the same time, the labor force had grown from 99.3 million workers in 1980 to 109 million workers by the end of 1985. Indeed, the Bureau of Labor Statistics reported that between 1983 and 1985 the investment-led economic recovery had produced more than 10 million new jobs — more than the entire continent of Europe had produced in the last decade.

And as day follows night, the healthy rise in the nation's GNP, the sharp rise in new job creation, and the subsequent drop in unemployment led in 1984 to the sharpest one-year decline in the poverty rate since 1973. According to the Bureau of the Census, the number of Americans at or below the poverty income line declined by 1.8 million people — a drop of nearly one full percentage point. "It's the fullest vindication of Mr. Reagan's thesis that it is economic growth, not social spending, that really fights poverty," said a lead editorial in the *Detroit News*.

All of this might have occurred faster and earlier had Congress not delayed the effective date of the tax cuts originally proposed by President Reagan. Though the tax cut bill was passed in 1981, it didn't fully take effect until two years later. In fact, because of the delay in effective implementation, taxes were cut by only 1.25 percent in 1981, a cumulative 10 percent in 1982, and a cumulative 20 percent in 1983. "The bulk of our tax cut began literally on January 1, 1983, and the economic recovery began at exactly the same time," observed economist Arthur B. Laffer, one of the primary architects of Reagan's supply-side tax cut proposal. "Isn't it amazing how tax cuts don't work until they take effect?"

Yet throughout this period, a large segment of the news media, a number of leading economic experts, and many of our most prominent political leaders were relentlessly forecasting only gloom and doom. Consider these dire warnings:

— "Mr Reagan's more radical advisers, led by Representative Jack Kemp of New York, want the three-year Kemp-Roth tax cut enacted immediately," the *New York Times* remarked on January 9, 1981. "They have an almost mystical faith that this would stimulate so much new production that the budget's imbalance would only be temporary and that, if monetary policy were held tight, rapid growth could proceed without a burst in new inflation. . . .

The supply-siders treat inflation too casually; their boldness is not justified by experience and their plan would almost certainly raise the already high expectation of more inflation."

— "It is not his [Reagan's] tenacity that is in question here but his wisdom," the *Times* continued on January 30, 1981. "For at a time when inflation is still untamed, such a tax cut risks making it worse."

— "[If the tax cut] does not create enough new revenues, by stimulating economic growth, to offset the revenue loss, the U.S. will be plunged into even a worse inflation than the double-digit price increases of the past two years," predicted Herbert W. Cheshire, editor of *Business Week* magazine on February 23, 1981.

— On February 26, the *Times* editorialized, "America, says President Reagan, needs a tax break to increase productivity. It is hard to disagree. But as the business economist Sam Nakagama puts it, the bang we can expect from the Reagan [tax cut] plan has 'all the potency of a popgun.' "

— "I know of no economic theory that says you can suppress monetary growth to fight inflation and simultaneously tune fiscal policy to spur growth," said Yale University economist William Nordhaus in July 1981.

— "The tax cuts are almost certain to boost consumption, while high interest rates will hold back investment," predicted Yale economist James Tobin in August 1981. "The result will be relatively feeble growth in productivity."

— "The theory that you can lick inflation by running a loose fiscal policy, cutting taxes heavily for individual taxpayers rather than skewing the reductions to stimulate investment, had a lot of political appeal, but it was always too good to be true," said President Jimmy Carter's former treasury secretary W. Michael Blumenthal in October 1981. "There never were any data to support the supply-side ideas . . . and the notion that somehow monetary policy can take up the slack without interest rates rising — and staying unacceptably high — was always no more than a dream."

And through it all, economists, politicians, and pundits alike kept insisting that tax increases were the cure-all for the economy's woes. "Given the size of the budget problem, i.e., the deficit, that exists, we may not be able to avoid actions to enlarge treasury receipts," i.e., raise taxes, said Milton W. Hudson of Morgan Guaranty Trust Company. "There is no way you can cut the budget enough," said economist Robert E. Lucas, Jr., of the University of Chicago. "We've got to reconsider the tax cuts." To which Joseph Pechman, economist at the Brookings Institution, added, "We have got to come up with more revenues."

These and other opponents of deep spending cuts and lower taxes warned repeatedly that if the tax cuts were not immediately repealed, the resulting higher deficits would push interest rates up even further, worsen inflation, and drive unemployment to new highs. Yet as the deficit mounted in the ensuing years — $79 billion in fiscal 1981, $128 billion in fiscal 1982, $208 billion in fiscal 1983, $185 billion in fiscal 1984, and $212 billion in fiscal 1985 — interest rates, unemployment, and inflation went down. The supply-side promises of increased economic growth with low inflation, more jobs, and lower interest rates were delivered, the *New York Times* notwithstanding. The doomsayers who called for taking more money out of the paychecks of Joe Lunchpail and the cash registers of Sam Businessman were proven dead wrong.

Critics of the 1981 tax cuts have steadfastly insisted that the rising deficit was the result of the tax cuts and not, as was the case, the result of massive increases in spending that rapidly outpaced ever-increasing federal revenues. But the proof is in the numbers. Federal tax revenues, which totaled $517.1 billion in 1980, rose to $666.5 billion in 1984, an increase of 28.89 percent. Federal outlays, by comparison, which totaled $591 billion in 1980, jumped to $852 billion by 1984 — a 44.1 percent increase. Clearly, the deficits came from too much spending, not from too little taxation.

America's economy went through a time of trial and testing during the Great Recession years, a time that I believe was a watershed in America's economic and political and social development. Yet despite our passage through the 1981–82 recession, the economy emerged in many ways stronger and more resilient than ever, thanks to the tax cuts, further deregulation of the economy, and, in the final analysis, a belief in the inherent strength of the marketplace to respond to incentives to invest, produce, and grow.

The revitalized economic growth of the 1980s, whose shaky beginnings were tempered in the fires of a severe recession, has blossomed forth into what I consider to be a new era of enterprise. America, says Harvard Business School professor Alfred D. Chandler, has entered its third entrepreneurial era. "The first was the second Industrial Revolution of the 1880s and '90s. The second was in the 1920s, when the great entrepreneurs, the Sloans and Fords, put together their giant enterprises."

I believe that the third entrepreneurial era, which gathered momentum in the late 1970s, really began to get a full head of steam in the 1980s. For it is in this decade that we have witnessed the great leap forward in new enterprises spawned by a deeper appreciation of the need to encourage growth through lower taxation, minimum regulation, and greater economic freedom. Although many interrelated economic, social, and political developments and changes preceded and in many ways contributed to the economic recovery and growth of the 1980s, it wasn't until the decade began that the politics of economic growth truly began to emerge, giving renewed voice to the promise of America.

The 1980s left behind a bearish and fearful presidential vision of an America sinking into a moral and economic malaise, a negative vision that foretold a future of limited growth and dwindling resources, a vision that proposed dividing the economic pie into smaller pieces and called upon Americans to lower their ambitions and their appetites for material goods and learn to do with less. Instead, the country bullishly turned, economically and politically, in the direction reflected by the supply-side themes struck by Ronald Reagan, New York congressman Jack Kemp, Georgetown University economist Paul Craig Roberts, and other disciples of limitless economic growth. It was a contagious view of America, one that struck deep, responsive chords in the American "can do" psyche. It is this philosophy of unlimited growth and expansion — based on the fundamental premise that people will never run out of resources because the most inexhaustible resource of all is knowledge — that has reignited a political, economic, and social revolution among millions of Americans and in the process has profoundly changed the United States for many years to come.

What we have today is a government of the rich, by the rich, and for the rich. . . . [President Reagan] gave each of his rich friends enough tax relief to buy a Rolls Royce — and he asked your family to pay for the hubcaps.

— *Walter Mondale*
July 20, 1984

An opportunity society awaits us. We need only believe in ourselves and give men and women of faith, courage, and vision the freedom to build it.

— *President Ronald Reagan*
March 2, 1984

CHAPTER 2

The Politics of Economic Growth

IN THE SPRING OF 1985, a London newspaper publisher made this comparison between the economic philosophy of many British working-class people and their counterparts in the United States: "In Great Britain," he said, "when a worker is walking down the street with his son and someone drives by in a Rolls Royce, he'll turn to his son and say, 'Look at that blankety blank rich capitalist living off the sweat of the workers.' But in the United States, if someone drives by in a Cadillac, the father is more apt to say to his son, 'If you work hard enough, someday you can have a car like that.' "

The comparison of working-class envy of those who attain wealth versus working-class ambition may be an overgeneralization about the differences between blue-collar workers here and in Great Britain. Yet there is within this story an important thread of truth that is deeply woven into the economic fabric of a can-do America. That belief and that spirit still live in America, and they are as much a part of our economic heritage as they are of our political heritage. That is why any discussion of America's new era of economic growth must include an examination of the political and social changes in this country that have not only pushed economic growth to the top of the national agenda but have profoundly changed the nation's political parties as well.

Ronald Reagan and his supporters, who won control of the White House in 1980 and retained power in 1984 — the first full, two-term president since Dwight Eisenhower — have clearly understood and effectively used the politics of economic growth, both to achieve power and to alter economic policy. Indeed, in his 1981 inaugural address, Reagan struck one of the central themes of his presidency: a nation of limitless potential and growth. "It is time for us to realize that we're too great a nation to limit ourselves to small dreams," he said. "We're not, as some would have us believe, doomed to an inevitable decline." Though cynics may say we live in an age when there are no heroes, Reagan's view is that "they just don't know where to look." The real heroes of America, he told the nation, are those who run the country's economy at every level of its structure — the factory workers, the food producers, the shopkeepers, and especially America's entrepreneurs — people who have "faith in themselves and faith in an idea, who create new jobs, new wealth, and opportunity."

One could search for years and never find a starker contrast between Reagan's economic vision of America and that of President Jimmy Carter and his vice-president, Walter Mondale, who failed to grasp the issues that formed the basis of economic growth and what Reagan called the opportunity society. Carter's and Mondale's policies and their campaign appeals were to a significant extent based on the envy of wealth, not the drive to attain it, an enmity toward business, not a shared alliance and commitment to its growth and success. Both virulently opposed tax rate reduction as a way to accelerate the economy's engine of growth. Neither expressed any understanding, appreciation, or wonderment at the irrepressible drive and determination that fuel America's entrepreneurial spirit. They failed to appeal to the dreams and the visions of all Americans to make a better life for themselves, for their children and their grandchildren.

Instead, in an extraordinarily nihilistic address to the nation in 1979, Carter told the American people that they had lost their way and that they were essentially to blame for America's problems; that they were suffering from "a crisis that strikes at the very heart and soul and spirit of our national will"; that this crisis was visible "in the growing doubt about the meaning of our own lives and in the loss of a unity of purpose for our nation"; that "the erosion of our confidence in the future is threatening to destroy the social and the political fabric of America"; and that "for the first time in the history of our country a majority of our people believe that the next five years will be worse than the past five years."

"I don't know any president who's ever misread public attitudes as dramatically as Carter did at that juncture," says Richard Wirthlin, President Reagan's pollster and issues strategist. Wirthlin should know, because throughout the 1980 and 1984 presidential campaigns, he privately conducted what he called focus group interviews in which he and his polltakers spent many hours in detailed conversation with small groups of Americans from all walks of life.

Wirthlin's close encounters sought to obtain a finer reading of what people were thinking about the issues, gathering the kind of first-hand observations and reactions that cold, clinical, national surveys often fail to obtain. In one of these sessions, Wirthlin vividly remembers a $12,000-a-year blue-collar worker in Provo, Utah, who was asked this question: "Should the government put more restrictions on businesses?" His blunt but clear response: "No, when business is good, businesses hire more workers and that gives me a better chance."

That view, expressed in a variety of ways in dozens of focus group interviews, confirmed, says Wirthlin, "the growing weight that people across the board put on business expansion and economic development and the degree to which they were intimately tied to their own economic survival and self-interest." Having gone through a painful recession in which layoffs were an everyday occurrence, in which workers and their unions voluntarily accepted pay freezes or cutbacks in order to keep their jobs and their companies afloat, Americans clearly had a deeper understanding and appreciation of the need for a vigorous and healthy business climate.

Congressman Jack Kemp of New York, whose enthusiastic economic growth philosophy deeply influenced the Reagan administration's politics and policies, wins understanding nods of approval when he tells audiences, "You can't have employees without employers." Obviously, policies that help businesses, large and small, to prosper will end up providing all Americans with more and better-paying jobs. Thus, the probusiness, economic growth views expressed in Wirthlin's encounter groups — a revalidation of President Calvin Coolidge's declaration that "the business of the American people is business" and John F. Kennedy's tax-cutting thesis that "a rising tide lifts all boats" — were pivotal public beliefs during Reagan's 1980 campaign for the presidency. And they became the linchpin around which Reagan spun his reelection strategy, a strategy in which he emphasized, as he had in 1980, the politics of economic growth — pounding away at the need for free market policies in Washington to help business to grow and prosper, to encourage entrepreneurs to take risks, and to offer working-class people the chance to climb the economic ladder of opportunity as far as it will take them.

However, while Reagan was pushing policies to strengthen the business sector and encourage the attainment of wealth, Walter Mondale, the 1984 Democratic presidential nominee, was campaigning against both of them. Like the British worker, Mondale appealed to the politics of envy instead of the politics of economic growth, deriding "the rich" and business a dozen times in his 1984 acceptance speech at the Democratic National Convention in San Francisco. He lashed out at "corporations" and criticized "big companies" and business executives who inhabit America's "boardrooms." To the average American employee who worked for a business, like the Provo, Utah, worker, Mondale seemed to be attacking the very enterprises that provided them with jobs, income, and the opportunity to get ahead. Worse, he was equating the very natural and human desire to keep more of one's income, and to attain economic security, with greed. "What kind of people are we?" he would ask audiences. Yet one could understand why Americans weren't exactly thrilled with Mondale's tax hike proposals, which would have raised taxes, beginning in 1985, for families with incomes over $25,000.

In stark contrast, Reagan appealed to the deepest economic motivations and drives of the American people — the belief that a person can accomplish anything and achieve anything if willing to work hard enough and long enough for it. "An opportunity society awaits us," he told an audience of supporters in 1984. "We need only believe in ourselves and give men and women of faith, courage, and vision the freedom to build it. Let others run down America and seek to punish success," he added. "Let them call you greedy for not wanting government to take more and more of your earnings. Let them defend their tombstone society of wage and price guidelines, mandatory quotas, tax increases, planned shortages, and shared sacrifices."

The economic growth themes that Reagan articulated so well in his presidential campaigns grew in large part from the careful polling Wirthlin had begun as early as 1978 — taking the pulse of America's economic and social values in preparation for Reagan's then unannounced 1980 campaign. Today, these surveys not only provide us with a broad outline of the public beliefs that made Ronald Reagan's election possible but also reveal the political and social underpinnings of the Era of Enterprise that blossomed and bore fruit in the 1980s.

In sharp contradiction to Jimmy Carter's famous "malaise" speech, Wirthlin's surveys discovered that the basic spirit of America was alive and well — just in need of a little morale boosting and leadership, that's all. Among other things, the polls showed that "Americans had not lost their spirit of adventure, their spirit that we can do anything we put our mind to; that there is a partnership between business and private citizens; and that it was government itself which was getting in the way and imposing burdens on both businesses and individuals and closing down rather than opening up opportunities."

"We did a series of value studies in that [1978–79] period," Wirthlin remembers, "primarily to answer the question, 'How can Reagan win in 1980?' He couldn't win by simply pulling in all the Republican votes. That would have given him about thirty-two to thirty-three percent of the vote. We had to look at blocks of voters who we could move en masse, and move from a thirty-three percent base to a fifty to fifty-five percent base. And we not only had to identify them but also find messages that Ronald Reagan strongly believed in that had the pulling power among those key groups.

"Now," Wirthlin continued, "it isn't surprising that Republicans, small businessmen, those with incomes above $35,000, believe in the can-do American society. But what did surprise us in 1978 and 1979, when we started to get ready for the election, was that that same belief that the frontier of America is an ever-expanding one and that Americans can lift themselves by their own bootstraps — if in fact they have opportunity and if government gets out of the way — was very strongly articulated among blue-collars, among Catholics, and among southerners. And those were the groups that we targeted primarily to get from the thirty-three percent to the fifty-two and fifty-three percent of the vote [in 1980]." And those were the very groups that made possible Reagan's election in 1980 as well as his reelection in 1984.

Reagan had four years to implement his programs and prove that his "opportunity society" prescriptions would work. Yet at the very time that he was encouraging free enterprise and economic risk taking as the solution to America's economic stagnation, pivotal economic attitudes were also changing and moving in Reagan's direction. Surveys by a number of professional polltakers, including Louis Harris and Daniel Yankelovich among others, clearly showed the sea change in economic attitudes that emerged in full force in the early 1980s. Consider these examples:

— In 1980 the Harris survey put this question to 1,202 Americans: "As you may know, the United States has been experiencing a sharp slowdown in the growth of productivity during the past few years. What this means is that the output per man-hour worked is less than what it used to be. I would like to read you several reasons that have been given to explain what has happened. For each, would you tell me if it is a very important reason, a somewhat important reason, a rather unimportant reason, or no reason at all for the decline in productivity growth." When the reason "excessive government regulation" was read, 41 percent answered "very important," 36 percent said "somewhat important," 11 percent replied "rather unimportant," 7 percent said "no reason at all," and 5 percent answered, "not sure." In other words, a convincing 77 percent saw excessive government regulation as a very important or somewhat important cause of the economy's poor productivity.

— In 1981 the Harris pollsters asked Americans what they thought of a number of specific federal economic subsidy programs that Reagan wanted to abolish. Included among them was the Economic Development Administration (EDA), a public works agency set up in the 1960s that has given billions of dollars in grants to localities in an effort to improve depressed local economies and combat unemployment. Yet studies have shown that these grants have had little if any effect. When asked what they thought of EDA, a stunning 65 percent said they favored abolishing it, 26 percent said they opposed abolition, and 9 percent weren't sure.

— Also in 1981, the Yankelovich pollsters submitted this sweeping antiregulatory statement to 1,221 randomly selected Americans: "The government should stop regulating business and protecting the consumer." A hefty 62 percent agreed with this statement, 32 percent disagreed, and 4 percent had no opinion.

— That same year, the Harris organization asked 1,201 Americans this question about the need for national economic planning by the government: "Some people believe that the best way to achieve economic growth is for government, business and labor to agree on a national economic plan and work together to achieve it. Others believe that business and labor should all pursue their own goals and interests and that a free market economy of this kind is the best way to achieve economic growth. Which of these comes closest to your own views?" An overwhelming 87 percent said they had faith in the free market route to achieve economic growth, while only 13 percent chose national economic planning.

By the 1984 presidential election year, when the economy had bounced back more vigorously than anyone had predicted, new surveys elicited two very important public opinions.

First, the American people more strongly than ever supported Reagan's generally free market prescriptions for strengthening the economy. Cutting taxes to leave more money in the cash registers of American businesses and the paychecks of America's workers clearly was the driving force that helped get the economy moving again. And public opinion surveys showed Americans overwhelmingly opposed to tax increases. Indeed, when the Gallup poll asked 1,590 randomly selected Americans if they favored or opposed tax increases to reduce the federal deficit, 62 percent said they were opposed versus 34 percent who favored higher taxes, with 4 percent registering no opinion. Notably, 65 percent of adults under the age of 30 registered strong opposition to tax increases.

Second, and equally important, Americans possessed renewed hope and greater optimism about future economic growth which, significantly, they correlated with Reagan's policies of tax cuts, deregulation, and spending restraints. Moreover, they saw such growth coming not from America's aging smokestack industries but from new and as yet unseen advances in high technology. For example:

— In an August 1984 NBC News/Associated Press poll, 2,400 Americans were asked, "Do you think the nation's economy has gotten better or worse since Ronald Reagan became president?" Sixty-two percent replied "better," 7 percent said "stayed the same," 26 percent said "worse," and 5 percent had no opinion.

— As the 1984 presidential election approached, a CBS News/*New York Times* poll in October 1984 asked 1,253 Americans if they thought "the economy will get worse" if either Reagan or Mondale was elected. The results showed that 57 percent thought the economy would *not* get worse if Reagan won, 31 percent thought it would, and 12 percent had no opinion. Forty-two percent thought the economy would get worse if Mondale won, 39 percent thought it wouldn't, and 19 percent had no opinion.

— A Harris poll commissioned for *Business Week* in June 1984 asked where "do you feel that future economic growth" will be coming from? Among those aged 20 to 36, the youth vote that in 1984 went heavily for Reagan, 72 percent answered "computers and high technology," 11 percent said "revitalization of old industries," and 15 percent replied "restrictions on imports from abroad." Among the 50-to-64 age group, 59 percent answered "computers and high technology," 13 percent said "revitalization of old industries," and 20 percent responded "restrictions on imports from abroad."

— The same Harris poll also raised this question about America's economic future: "Thinking beyond this current period, if you had to say, over the next twenty years, do you feel that the economy in this country will have a slower rate of growth than in the past, or do you feel that economic growth will be almost unlimited as a result of technological and scientific advances?" Among people between the ages of 20 and 36, a bullish 52 percent foresaw "unlimited growth," while 42 percent saw "slower growth." Among the 50-to-64 age group, 46 percent expected "unlimited growth," and 43 percent saw slower growth ahead.

Obviously, many factors contributed to Ronald Reagan's reelection in 1984 with 59 percent of the popular vote and 525 electoral votes, more electoral votes than anyone had ever before won in U.S. history. The economy had substantially recovered from the recession, and people attributed much of the recovery to Reagan's economic policies; the electorate, according to a number of nationwide surveys, had grown increasingly conservative and thus had moved closer to Reagan's political views;* and there was also a feeling that the country had finally shaken off the seemingly endless crises and national self-doubt that had plagued it throughout the 1960s and 1970s, and Reagan was to some extent associated with this, too. But the most significant and overriding reason behind Ronald Reagan's rise to power, and his overwhelming reelection at the age of 73, was his emphasis on economic growth initiatives to strengthen the private sector, motivate new business formations, create more jobs, and expand economic opportunity for all Americans.

*The Harris survey reported in March 1986 that for the first time since 1968 more Americans called themselves conservative than moderate. Forty percent defined themselves as conservative, 38 percent were moderates, and only 18 percent were liberal. A decade ago, 31 percent called themselves conservative, 40 percent described themselves as moderates, and 18 percent said they were liberals.

Reagan, however, did not originate the politics of economic growth. He had merely popularized and polished it through his speeches and his policies — though it was a natural extension of his long-held beliefs in free enterprise and free market economics. Others before him, such as presidents Franklin Delano Roosevelt and John F. Kennedy, had made economic growth the pivotal issue in their political agendas and in the process made their party the majority political party for more than five decades. Reagan not only borrowed their emphasis on getting the nation moving again, but took great delight in quoting from them at length in his speeches.

There is much in the policies and postures of these two activist presidents that Reagan and his supply-side political allies strongly identified with. For example, Roosevelt flatly rejected the advice of Hoover Republicans, who in the 1930s were calling for the same thing that many Democrats were proposing in the early 1980s, namely that taxes be raised to eliminate the government's deficit. And nowhere in his presidential addresses did FDR better delineate his opposition to balancing the budget through tax increases than in a 1936 campaign address in which he said this:

"The money to run the government comes from taxes; and the tax revenue depends for its size on the size of the national income. When the incomes and the values and transactions of the country are on the down-grade, then tax receipts go on the down-grade too. If the national income continues to decline, then the government cannot run without going into the red. The only way to keep the government out of the red is to keep the people out of the red. And so we [have] to balance the budget of the American people before we [can] balance the budget of the national government. That makes sense doesn't it? *To pile on vast new taxes would get us nowhere because values [would go] down, and that makes sense too.*" (Emphasis added.)

John F. Kennedy went one giant step further by championing tax cuts as the way to spur growth and "get America moving again," and his cuts did just that, achieving full employment without inflation. "That's where we got the idea of cutting tax rates across the board," says Congressman Jack Kemp, who with Senator William Roth of Delaware had been beating the drums throughout the 1970s for tax cuts to stimulate economic growth. They sold their Kemp-Roth tax rate reduction plan to Reagan in 1980 at a time when the economy was rapidly worsening and the nation, not to mention the Republican party, was looking for answers to breathe new life into an anemic economy. It only remained for Reagan, who quickly grasped the populist potential of the long dormant issue of economic growth, to tap its political and economic power.

Thus, in an ironic political flipflop, a half century after the New Deal began, America's two great parties switched positions on the fundamental economic issue of our times. The Democratic party of FDR and JFK, who understood not only the important role of economic growth in funding the social programs they supported, but also how counterproductive tax increases could be to economic expansion, had suddenly donned the clothing of the Hoover Republicans, crying for tax increases to solve America's economic problems. This was something akin to a seventeenth-century physician prescribing bloodletting to stop acute hemorrhaging. At the same time, Reagan and the Republicans were suddenly quoting FDR and JFK every chance they got, declaring that raising taxes to balance the budget, as Democratic leaders were then proposing, was the surest way to put both the people and the government, as FDR said, deeper into the red. The two parties had completely abandoned their traditional positions on fiscal policy. The Democratic party was pushing draconian taxation and further austerity, while the Republicans were calling for expanding the economic pie and thus improving the revenue flow into Washington as well as into the paychecks of the American people.

In the final analysis, Ronald Reagan's successful pursuit of the presidency, as Richard Wirthlin detailed it in a 1980 symposium at Harvard University's Kennedy School of Politics, was driven by seven key imperatives, which were the pivotal issues of his campaign. The first and most important imperative was "that we place trust in the values of American society which were largely responsible for sustaining its growth." But if this imperative represented the heart of the politics of economic growth, the next imperative was its soul: "That the sluggish economy and inflation are principally caused by excessive government spending, taxation, and regulation." Both of these imperatives, Wirthlin's polls showed, were tightly woven into the fabric of American political opinion.

Thus, in a much larger sense, Reagan's successful 1980 campaign against Jimmy Carter was a fortunate juncture between the man and the moment, between Reagan's free market beliefs and a sea change in American politics and attitudes that was occurring throughout key sectors of society. Says Wirthlin: "I think Americans by 1980 had pretty well rejected many of the old assumptions that drove the New Deal agenda — i.e., that government could be an equal participant and could facilitate not only the stabilization of the economy through Keynesian fiscal policies but also could do it in a humanitarian fashion which would give those who are less fortunate in society more opportunity.

"By 1980," he continues, "we had both inflation and unemployment, which flew directly into the face of the Keynesian proposition. And many, many Americans came to the conclusion that in spite of spending billions and billions of dollars on the Great Society, the poor weren't being helped, but the middle class and the lower middle class were carrying a very heavy burden in trying to use government as a mechanism to drive social change. What's happened since that time is that people have had four years to assess the Reagan agenda and have pretty well come to accept even more strongly the precepts of a growth society, namely everyone is better off if the society grows. And the corollary to that is that government itself doesn't generate growth, but it is the millions of individuals and small businesses and corporations who innovate, induce change, hire people, and stimulate the economy."

Numerous social, educational, demographic, and attitudinal factors have contributed to this political change. Certainly, one of the most significant factors in the late 1970s and early 1980s has been on our college campuses. Where once "Big Business" was frequently ridiculed and criticized by much of academia, and capitalism made the whipping boy for all of society's ills, now economics departments are increasingly being staffed by a new and younger generation of free market economists. The fact that President Reagan, the most conservative American president in the last half century, could look in 1982 to Harvard University, long a bastion of

Eastern liberalism and Keynesian economic thinking, for the chairman of his Council of Economic Advisers, Dr. Martin Feldstein, a free marketeer, suggests that much has changed on our college campuses. The economics departments of colleges and universities both large and small are becoming increasingly diversified, with more and more of their faculty members championing free market to libertarian viewpoints. And school and college administrators have been aggressively responding to the entrepreneurial explosion, adding to their curriculums innovative new courses to better prepare tomorrow's business leaders. The number of colleges offering programs and courses on starting a new business has skyrocketed from 8 to more than 150 since 1967, with much of the growth occurring in the first half of the 1980s.

Says Dr. Richard Rahn, chief economist for the U.S. Chamber of Commerce: "The schools whose reputations are increasing are much more the free market schools. The most notable example is George Mason University in northern Virginia, which by many accounts already has one of the ten best economics departments in the country. But even in some of the old-line bastions of liberalism, they now feel obligated to hire at least the token free marketeer. And the students seem to be more influenced by these people than the old statist professors. I see the change in terms of the job applications, people seeking jobs here. People wander in from good schools, from old-line schools, who are free marketeers. I get people in here who did their graduate work at Harvard and perhaps they didn't get it so much from their professors, but they have a strong commitment to the free market when they walk in here. A few years ago that was not the case."

Career attitudes also have been changing, with more and more young people deciding on careers in business, and fewer people choosing to study such subjects as sociology and urban problems, which were popular fifteen or twenty years ago. By the beginning of the 1980s, the business schools were experiencing record-breaking enrollments. According to the U.S. Department of Education, more than 133,000 persons graduated from colleges and universities with bachelor's degrees in business and management in 1975, representing 14.4 percent of the 922,933 bachelor's degrees awarded that year. By 1983, however, the number of business graduates had shot up to a robust 226,892, representing 23.4 percent of all bachelor's degree graduates. That figure continues to climb higher. Today, nearly one-fourth of all undergraduate degrees are in the field of business.

At the same time, public attitudes toward basic, bread-and-butter economic issues — traditionally high on the list of major concerns among Americans — have intensified and grown stronger. A 1985 survey of economic attitudes by the National Association of Home Builders, for example, found that the American dream of homeownership "still ranks as a top priority among most Americans, especially young households still trying to buy their first homes." The survey found that housing was the fourth highest personal priority, just behind good health, job security, and financial independence. Significantly, buying a home ranked first among 25-to-34-year-olds. Pocketbook issues generally were of "most concern" to the average American — with cutting the deficit and unemployment the most frequently cited.

There are those who will insist that the politics of economic growth is just a passing national fad in the political cycle, and that it is only a matter of time until it will be eclipsed by a new kind of politics, perhaps a return to more economic planning and regulation, and sharply increased taxes. But the continuing national public opinion surveys that relentlessly take the pulse of the nation suggest that this isn't going to happen anytime soon, if at all; that the desire for vigorous economic growth cuts across all demographic and political lines; and that the politics of growth, as a political movement and an economic philosophy, has just begun. This belief is certainly supported by a 1985 Gallup survey that found considerable opposition to certain economic regulations by government, or at least a desire to modify them significantly, and a growing opposition to higher taxes.

For example, should the minimum wage laws be changed so that teenagers 19 and under can be paid a subminimum wage of $2.50 per hour for the summer months in order to reduce high youth unemployment, particularly in our inner cities? Fifty-seven percent of those polled answered yes, while 43 percent said no. Should federal taxes be raised to cut the deficit? An overwhelming 76 percent said no, 18 percent said yes, and 6 percent had no opinion.

The politics of economic growth is here to stay, long into the foreseeable future, because it has become an intraparty phenomenon, forming the heart and soul of today's Republican party, and becoming an increasing force for change within the Democratic party as well. Certainly, the two leading political exponents of economic growth policies and initiatives within the two major parties, aside from Ronald Reagan himself, are Congressman Jack Kemp, a conservative Republican from New York, and Senator Bill Bradley, a liberal to moderate Democrat from New Jersey. Both Kemp and Bradley represent the younger generation of their parties and both have substantial influence within them. Both are deeply, almost religiously, fervent in their economic growth beliefs — and they find much on which to agree, from tax rate reduction to international monetary reform.

"I worship at the altar of economic growth," Kemp says of his political beliefs. "I come from a small-business background, so I've got a bias toward new enterprise, and kind of a George Gilder view that the country's driven by *new* enterprises, not established enterprises. I'm not *anti*–big business, but my populism aims itself at encouraging a higher degree of entrepreneurship."

Kemp was the arch-exponent of supply-side economics in Congress in the late 1970s, his thinking heavily influenced by a band of economic thinkers and writers including Jude Wanniski, a former editorial writer for the *Wall Street Journal;* California economist Arthur Laffer; Irving Kristol, editor of the neoconservative journal *The Public Interest;* and then-congressman David Stockman of Michigan, who later broke with Kemp on supply-side economics. Largely self-taught on economics, Kemp steeped himself in economic growth issues and prescriptions and became a major force for tax cuts and other growth initiatives, deeply influencing Reagan's views and the policies of his administration.

Kemp believes in the lowest tax rates possible on income to provide the greatest incentives possible to work, save, invest, and produce. And it was his tax rate reduction proposal, with some modification, that became the law of the land in 1981 and that helped lead the economy out of the Great Recession. Moreover, Kemp's economic views have won the allegiance of a number of bright young Republican activists in Congress who have organized themselves into the thirty-five-member Conservative Opportunity Society caucus, headed by Congressman Newt Gingrich of Georgia. Together they have not only changed the political posture of their party but also — through their speeches, articles, and books — deeply influenced the views of Americans from all walks of life.

On the other hand, spend an hour talking to Bill Bradley and you will soon understand why his voice is the future of the Democratic party. Though Bradley may be on the other side of the aisle from Kemp and represent a minority voice within his party, his economic views are virtually synonymous with Kemp's. While his party's presidential ticket stumped the country in 1984 excoriating business and the wealthy, and calling for tax increases for the very people who save and invest most, Bradley was saying just the opposite: the way toward a more prosperous economy is not to raise taxes but to cut them, he insists. "The Democratic party should be emphasizing economic growth as the key to fulfilling our promises to the elderly and the disadvantaged, as the key to increasing our competitiveness in the world economy, as the key to bringing everybody to the higher ground," he says. "We need to get maximum incentives for people to work and to save. I think the greatest incentive for saving and investment is the lowest possible rate of tax on profit." Ronald Reagan and Jack Kemp couldn't have said it better.

Like Kemp, Bradley authored a tax reform plan in the early 1980s with a close ally, Congressman Richard Gephardt of Missouri, another Democratic crusader for economic growth initiatives. The plan — which Bradley and Gephardt unsuccessfully tried to get Mondale to endorse in 1984 — called for lowering the tax rates to a maximum of 35 percent and eliminating loopholes. "If you eliminate those loopholes," Bradley says, "you can lower the rates because you end up getting more revenues, which encourages work, savings, and investment." Lowering tax rates further obviously was not the economic philosophy espoused by Walter Mondale, the Democratic party's titular political leader, nor by most of the party's congressional leaders. The party, Bradley admits, is in a period of "ferment, defining itself in terms of the emerging realities of the world." In what direction would he like to see his party turn? To a more centrist position on economic policy, "consistent with what Jack Kennedy did."

Democratic Young Turks like Bradley and Gephardt are their party's future and its hope. It is only a matter of time until they ascend to the party's leadership and begin molding its policies. But for now their economic growth efforts are clearly beginning to influence the direction in which the Democratic party is headed, just as Jack Kemp and Ronald Reagan have deeply influenced the direction in which their party has traveled.

"We started with just a tiny number of people challenging the whole established order," says Jude Wanniski, who remains one of Kemp's chief economic advisers. "Our objective as revolutionaries was not to win offices, not to win a presidency or a specific senate seat or governorship. Our objective was to change the whole order of things so that all the candidates are supply-siders." Political candidates are far from being all supply-siders, yet by the mid-1980s the politics of economic growth had undeniably changed the whole order of things.

We have lived through the age of big industry and the age of the giant corporation. But I believe that this is the age of the entrepreneur.

— *President Ronald Reagan*

The man with a new idea is a crank — until the idea succeeds.

— *Mark Twain*

CHAPTER 3

The Age of the Entrepreneur

THEY ARE AMERICA'S IDEA MAKERS and risk takers. They dream great dreams and make them come true. They create something out of nothing. They make things happen. They bring people together to build an economic organization that produces income, creates jobs, launches careers, nurtures families, funds philanthropies, and provides for the common good. They overcome personal insecurities, naysayers, financial adversity, and fierce competition — and the best of them survive. They daringly create products and services for which there is often no demonstrable need and then set about to produce a demand for what they're selling. They are part dreamer, part promotor, part inventor, part salesperson, part Samaritan, part psychologist, part evangelist, part army sergeant, and part adventurer. They know how to turn a dollar, meet a payroll, and find a market for their goods. Their leadership can inspire loyalty, ignite an explosion of awesome inventiveness and mind-boggling technology, and motivate hard work and record-breaking productivity. They are authentic American heroes.

They are entrepreneurs, a special breed of people who help make America grow.

Their rags-to-riches stories are at once endlessly fascinating, infectious, and inspiring to all who seek to emulate them and create a successful, prosperous enterprise of their own. From sea to shining sea they come forth in seemingly inexhaustible numbers, people of all ages and from all classes, native Americans and immigrants, millionaires and paupers, young and old, to write their names across the signboards of new industries and new enterprises, big and small. Consider these remarkable examples:

— When Frederick W. Smith was an undergraduate at Yale in the mid-1960s, he wrote a paper for an economics class outlining his idea for a company that would provide next-day delivery service across the country for letters and packages that "absolutely, positively have to be there overnight." The company, he wrote, would have its own fleet of jets and vans and deliver parcels anywhere in the United States. Smith's professor gave him a C on his paper, but in the early 1970s, at the age of 27, he turned his vision into Federal Express, which for a mere $11 will jet your letter or package anywhere in the country and personally deliver it to its destination by ten-thirty the next morning. At first, Smith's losses were high, $29 million in the first two years of operation, largely as a result of high energy prices triggered by the 1973 Arab oil embargo. But after that his company's revenues rose steadily. Today, Federal Express delivers 450,000 packages and letters a night; the company grossed $1.4 billion in revenues in 1984, earning post-tax profits totaling $115 million.

— Consider Pierre and Deland deBeaumont, a husband-and-wife team who at age 50 started selling hard-to-find home tools and "fiendishly ingenious devices" by mail from a kitchen table in their eighteenth-century farmhouse in Pittsfield, Massachusetts. They ran their first ad in *Workbench* magazine and began some modest direct mail advertising, and the orders began rolling in. When other couples their age might be thinking of retirement, the deBeaumonts worked fifteen-hour days, seven days a week. From the beginning, each day's orders were shipped out the same day, or no later than the next morning. The company prospered, reaching $300,000 in annual sales in four years. Like all successful entrepreneurs, they had a "unique selling point" that no one else in the marketplace was offering. They offered tools and household gadgets that people couldn't find in local hardware stores — a special clamp to hold together pieces of a dollhouse chair, a screwdriver to take apart watches, or a tool to reset the teeth of a handsaw at a perfectly accurate angle. Fifteen years later, in 1980, having expanded into gourmet cookware, housekeeping products, and other items, this industrious couple sold their hugely successful mail order company, Brookstone, to the Quaker Oats Company for $9 million.

— The world was full of companies making sneakers whose soles all looked generally alike until Philip Knight pressed some rubber against his wife's waffle iron to create a new waffle sole that produced one of his company's most popular products and helped make Nike, Inc., a pioneer in the athletic footwear industry. Knight was majoring in business at the University of Oregon in 1958 when, as an accomplished runner, he got to know Oregon's famous track coach Bill Bowerman. Bowerman, who complained that American running shoes were too clunky and heavy for runners seeking to set new world records, knew a thing or two about designing better, faster footwear. Later, after Knight graduated from Stanford, he and Bowerman pooled their resources and ordered a Japanese firm to make them three hundred pairs of Tiger running shoes, which they began selling largely in the western states. Nike, Inc., was started. Their specially designed running shoes were used successfully in the 1972 Olympic trials, and their company was poised to take advantage of the jogging craze that took off in the mid-1970s. Knight's brilliant marketing savvy, plus his ability to locate new suppliers in Taiwan, Japan, South Korea, Malaysia, Thailand, and the Philippines, made his line of athletic shoes the most competitive in the United States. He even helped boost our own sagging shoe industry by establishing factories in Exeter, New Hampshire, and Saco, Maine. Today, Nike is a $946.4 million-a-year-business, employing 1,900 workers in the United States.

— In 1971 Nolan Bushnell, son of a Utah cement contractor, invented a new video game called Pong, which resembles Ping-Pong and was the first successful coin-operated game of its kind. A passionate tinkerer in electronics and computers, Bushnell developed the game in 1971 while a student at the University of Utah and began marketing Pong in 1972. He founded a company with the Japanese name of Atari, which means "warning." The almost-overnight success of Pong, and related games, revolutionized the arcade industry, which was then largely made up of pinball machine games. Four years later, he sold Atari to Warner Communications for $28 million, only to immediately plunge into an entirely different entrepreneurial field by starting a nationwide chain of Chuck E. Cheese Pizza Time Theaters, an enterprise that took off and showed enormous promise, only to fold in 1984.

— In 1979 Lorraine Mecca, a former junior high school English teacher, risked $25,000 she got from selling her house before moving in with her new Hungarian-born husband, to launch a microcomputer hardware and software company in Fountain Valley, California. Six years later her company, Micro D, was selling computerware to over 4,000 retailers nationwide, with sales exceeding $120 million in 1984. When Micro D went public in 1983, Mecca's holdings were worth an estimated $59 million. "I had worked for a number of other people," she says, "and didn't feel that I was always appreciated or got to do many of the things I thought I was capable of doing."

She learned about the computer retail business through her husband, who with an associate ran two computer stores. By attending monthly meetings of the Southern California Computer Dealers Association, she discovered that many retailers had difficulty obtaining software supplies as well as modems and printers. Sensing a big need in the computer market that was not being filled, she started a distribution company in her home, wholesaling computer products that were compatible with Apple, and later with IBM computers. She was a month into her business when her husband sold out to his associate and joined the fledgling enterprise. Their company rang up $3.5 million in revenues in its first year of operation, and since then there has been no looking back. Micro D now has branches in Chicago, Dallas, and Columbia, Maryland.

— Morris Siegel, 35, who never went to college, has been described as "a guy with the moral conviction of Abraham Lincoln, the drive of Lee Iacocca, and the whimsy of E.T." He started his Celestial Seasonings Company in 1971 with an herbal tea that he and his wife harvested in the foothills of the Rocky Mountains near Boulder, Colorado. By the time he was 26, Mo Siegel's company was marketing its products in stores across the country and he was a millionaire. Celestial Seasonings now produces twenty-seven varieties of herbal tea, packaged in colorful cartons, in addition to herbal shampoos and conditioners under the brand name Mountain Herbery. Between 1978 and 1983, his sales tripled, reaching $27 million. His firm of more than two hundred employees is nonunion and refuses to install time clocks. Tacked on the wall of his plant is a sign that reads, "Price, Quality, Speed — Pick Any 2."

From Steven Jobs, the young computer whiz who invented the personal computer in his garage and founded the Apple Computer corporation, to Wally "Famous" Amos, an unemployed black theatrical agent who reinvented the ultra-rich chocolate chip cookie, America is a land of, by, and for entrepreneurs. Indeed, many business experts and economists believe that the United States is undergoing an entrepreneurial revolution. This was the conclusion reached in 1985 by *Inc.* magazine, one of many business journals spawned in this era of enterprise, when it celebrated the news that America's entrepreneurs had created a record-shattering 634,991 new businesses in 1984. "The small and mid-sized business sector has become so dynamic, in fact, that an estimated eighty-two percent of the two million new jobs being created this year [1985] will come from companies having nine hundred and ninety-nine or fewer employees," says *Inc.* publisher Bernard A. Goldhirsh, and the vast majority of these were firms of one hundred employees or less. Not only did a record three million new businesses get started in the first four years of the 1980s, but the odds of their survival increased dramatically as well. "The old myth that nine out of ten new businesses fail just isn't viable anymore," says *Inc.* editor George Gendron. In sum, says Professor Peter Drucker of California's Claremont Graduate School, a widely respected expert in business management, "We have on our hands an entrepreneurial boom the like of which we have not seen in a century. The most important economic event of the last few years, in fact, is the emergence of this entrepreneurial trend."

The creators of these small to mid-sized companies come in all shapes and sizes and philosophies, starting their enterprises for a wide variety of reasons. And sometimes making a fortune is the least of them. When Joel Hyatt began Hyatt Legal Services nine years ago at the age of 27, "it was really idealism that caused me to start it, much less than a self-perception of being an entrepreneur." His dream, born out of his idealism and his liberalism, was to make legal services affordable for middle- to lower-income people. But once his enterprise got off the ground, "I very quickly learned that I better be a good entrepreneur or I wouldn't be able to turn the idea into a meaningful reality, I wouldn't be able to make it economically viable, I wouldn't be able to make it work." But make it work he did, and today Hyatt Legal Services is the largest law firm in the United States, with over two hundred locations across the country, in thirty-one of the top forty markets. It serves about 300,000 new clients a year, about 45 percent of whom have never seen a lawyer before, and it's still growing. He says he's "just scratching the surface of fulfilling the need" for low-cost legal services. Hyatt's idea of a national chain of law offices not only launched a radically new concept of making legal services widely affordable, but it also changed Joel Hyatt's views on the private sector, entrepreneurs, and economic growth as well.

For Hyatt, an honors graduate of Dartmouth and Yale Law School and a product of the liberal activism of the 1960s and 1970s, going into business and becoming a capitalist was the farthest thing from his mind — as it was for a lot of kids during this period. Unlike other entrepreneurs, who acquired much of their entrepreneurial instinct from their parents, Hyatt says his father, who was in the umbrella business, "was unhappy with his own business career. He never once encouraged me to pursue business. To him, business was always a very distasteful thing. He disliked business immensely." Instead, he wanted his son to become a lawyer and pursue a career in public service.

"As long as I can remember, I'd always wanted to be a lawyer, and to be involved in something in the public arena. It really was kind of a surprise that I became an entrepreneur." After law school, he worked first in the prestigious New York City law firm of Paul, Weiss, Rifkind, Wharton, and Garrison for Ted Sorensen, former counsel to President John F. Kennedy. In 1976 he helped run the senatorial campaign of Ohio Democrat Howard Metzenbaum, who is his father-in-law and one of the most liberal members of the U.S. Senate, well known for his blistering political attacks on the business community.

In 1977, however, he founded Hyatt Legal Services in Cleveland, with his wife, Susan, serving as a senior partner. The concept was clean and simple and the market was wide open: a series of small, efficient, low-cost offices, opened nights and Saturdays, and charging standard fees for divorces ($375 if uncontested, $675 if contested), simple wills ($55), adoptions ($300), bankruptcy, and other legal problems. "I wanted to be a people's lawyer," he said. "I wanted to develop a mechanism whereby a large segment of our population who never had access to legal services would be able to obtain such access." His targeted market was the middle 70 percent of the population, which, studies showed, was not being adequately served by the legal profession. This group, as Hyatt describes it, was "not poor enough to qualify for free government-funded legal aid and not wealthy enough to afford the traditional law firms, which have always served the affluent."

He and his wife, Susan, worked seven days a week from morning until late at night to make their concept work. As with many fledgling businesses, Hyatt's biggest problem was with the bank where he had taken out a major loan. It was a demand note, and as his business struggled to find its market and gain a foothold, the bankers began to get nervous. "They had my signature and my partner's signature, and we were worth at the time about twelve dollars, if that." One day a bank official asked to see him, saying, "Mr. Hyatt, we're very concerned about how your business is developing. Please let us know within seven days how you're going to repay the note." Hyatt replied, "Look, you have a demand note. If you want to call it, call it. That will put us under, and you'll get nothing, which strikes me as a very stupid thing to do." The banker answered, "Mr. Hyatt, we presume rational behavior on your part," to which Hyatt replied, "You presume whatever the hell you want," and walked out of his office. The loan was not called.

What would he have done if the bank had called his loan? "I don't have the slightest idea, because you never think of it. I mean, failure is not a word that is in the vocabulary of an entrepreneur. And when I played that bluff, I didn't have the foggiest notion. Even when I went home that night and had a sleepless night, it wasn't because I was trying to think what I'd do if they called that loan. I can't explain it to you, it's all emotional, but you never think what you're doing isn't going to work. I would have had to reach the point of saying, 'Well, they're going to call my bluff, they're going to call the loan, now what am I going to do for the money?' But you know, I never got to that point. You're just certain that what you're doing is going to work."

The birth of Hyatt's new enterprise was timed perfectly with a 1978 Supreme Court decision that for the first time allowed attorneys to advertise — though Hyatt's arguments before the Ohio Supreme Court resulted in Ohio's becoming the first state to allow lawyers to advertise on radio and television. Handsome, articulate, and personable, Hyatt used television to personally sell his service to the masses, ending each spot with the promise, "You've got my word on it." The market he targeted with his television pitches was "a fairly large segment of the public that was afraid of lawyers, that feared the cost of lawyers, that didn't know where to go for certain kinds of legal services. We were presenting a new kind of law firm with a new image. And the public's response to that was overwhelmingly positive." Thus, he joined a steady stream of mass medium entrepreneurs, like Remington shaver's Victor Kiam, Chrysler's Lee Iacocca, and that ultimate chicken salesman Maryland's Frank Perdue, who made a personal appeal to old-fashioned values such as trustworthiness and honesty to show that they stood behind their products and guaranteed them.

Then in 1980 Hyatt joined forces with H&R Block, Inc., of Kansas City, Missouri, the nationwide tax preparers, to form a new H&R Block subsidiary, Block Management Company. The new subsidiary provides Hyatt's firm with a wide range of administrative, marketing, and real estate services — including computer processing, advertising, accounting, and even furnishing and equipping offices as the Hyatt company expands. Block, whose hugely successful company processes over 10 million tax reports a year, saw a gold mine in Hyatt's idea. By attending to these support functions for Hyatt, Block allows the company to concentrate on what it does best, provide legal services, and in the process to accelerate its nationwide expansion.

It is significant that Hyatt came out of an educational and political period in which many students thought that the best way to fight poverty was to become a VISTA volunteer or a social worker or help grow rice in Southeast Asia. Becoming a businessman was viewed with disdain by many politically liberal students, who were given little if any education in how the marketplace and capitalism can be a force to eliminate poverty and to improve society. Those kinds of attitudes are changing and so, in some ways, has Joel Hyatt. "I'm a product of an activist sixties and seventies in terms of when I went to college and to law school. No one that I knew then was talking about being an entrepreneur," he says. "That clearly has changed. Today, there's almost a cult about entrepreneurship. Lots of college kids really want to become entrepreneurs." When he was invited to speak at a conference at Stanford on entrepreneurship, "I was amazed at how many hundreds of young people came to attend the conference over the weekend to learn how to become an entrepreneur. But I think there's some good coming from that and, you know, I believe it really is the entrepreneur who is creating economic growth in the country, who is creating jobs, and clearly one of our most important societal challenges is to create jobs." He believes that the United States "in the last five years" has entered a new entrepreneurial age. "I think we're seeing some of the benefits of that.

"And I've come to believe, too, that in terms of our social agenda, we really can't do as much as we should in this society unless we're a growing society. So I've come to be a much stronger believer in the importance of entrepreneurial activity, the potential that it holds out, indeed, even to the point of believing that a lot of society's problems can be dealt with in the private sector. I think Hyatt

Legal Services is an excellent example of that. There was a very critical problem about access to legal counseling on the part of middle-income people. And we're a good example of a private sector initiative that addressed that important social problem. And we're doing it within the context of the free enterprise system. So I believe much more today than I did as a college student in the potential for the private sector to identify and address social problems." What kind of social problems? Well, take the problem of providing access to the legal system for the poor, says Hyatt. The federal government does that through the $300 million-a-year Legal Services Corporation, "but quite candidly I think that it's not nearly as good a program as the private sector can do."

Hyatt's experience has also taught him some valuable lessons about the kinds of regulatory obstacles that await almost all entrepreneurs, including lawyers. In his case, "There are regulations governing the practice of law which I think still create unnecessary barriers." For example, state bar associations "have too many regulations that seek to limit competition. That's what the advertising regulations used to do. They didn't want to advertise because they didn't want competition."

For many entrepreneurs, the excitement is in creating and building an enterprise, not necessarily in running it forever. The challenge is gone for some after they've built their organization, and they get an itch to start something new. "I think in the dynamic of really any organization, there are different abilities and talents that go into building it than running it. [Hyatt Legal Services is] still at what I call the entrepreneurial stage of development. We're still building it." But "at some point I think we'll be at a stage where we have to be run as opposed to built. I think that will take different talents and abilities. At that point in our organization's life, I'm likely to pursue some other challenges."

The secret of Hyatt's success? Many factors, to be sure, but one stands out. "I think it's determination. Almost every entrepreneur will tell you that they started with an idea, that everyone else told them it couldn't work, but they just didn't believe it. That's certainly true in my case, and it's true in many of the really successful entrepreneurial ideas out there. I mean, no one thought that this little computer being built in the garage, that anybody was going to buy a personal computer. That's true of so many different situations that create an industry. And, frankly, that's what we've done within the legal profession. We've created a new industry and no one thought it would work. And I think that a common theme among entrepreneurs is that they have a different vision. They just don't buy the conventional notions.

"Anyone without that level of fortitude and determination is never going to take an idea and make anything of it. You have to be able to have the discipline to create a plan, to create a game plan. You have to be able to think what resources you're going to need. You have to be organized. You have to be systematic and you have to be disciplined. I think you have to combine the vision of a dreamer with the pragmatism of a realist. So that what you're doing is translating your vision into reality, and you're doing that by hard work, by planning. You're not just dreaming. That's the difference between the successful entrepreneur and dreamers."

Or consider the entrepreneurial creativity of David Liederman, a rotund, mustachioed ex-lawyer who apprenticed as a chef in a three-star French restaurant and wrote a best-selling cookbook before launching his $40 million-a-year cookie business, David's Cookies, with more than one hundred thirty stores both here and abroad. The chief advantage of owning your own company, he says, is not having to go through committees to make decisions. "I have marketing meetings in the shower every morning."

Liederman humbly describes himself as "a working stiff" who dreams up his own products and listens to children instead of overpaid marketing researchers. Yet behind that "Aw, shucks, I just bake cookies for a living" demeanor, he has international visions of cookie exports helping to make Americans proud of American products again. Having conquered the U.S. market, he quickly cast his eyes overseas. "You can't get much more American than the chocolate chip cookie," he says enthusiastically. "Foreigners love American food concepts and they seem to be buying the stuff." In Japan, where David's Cookies "is doing real well," Kentucky Fried Chicken and McDonald's are the top two restaurant firms. China, too, may one day give David's a chance, if Liederman can figure out "what the politics are to get in."

When David's Cookies began in New York in 1980, "American food was a dirty word" in Europe, he says. "Now everything has turned American. Restaurants have American flags in them and people are serving hamburgers and ribs and pizza. It's good for our side, because at least we have something to export once in a while." To the doubters who have been overfed on America's inability to compete overseas, he argues that "people vote with their pocketbooks." At McDonald's in Paris "there always seems to be a long line out the door. If the French hate McDonald's, what are they standing in line for?"

Like aggressive entrepreneurs everywhere, Liederman works constantly to expand his enterprise wherever there are potential customers. He continues to add to the number of retail outlets here and abroad that offer more than a dozen kinds of cookies in addition to the basic chocolate chunk cookie that got him started and made his company a worldwide success. He has also begun to diversify into the noncookie line. His latest brainstorm: muffins with gigantic tops. According to Liederman's Great Muffin Theory, people like the tops best, and he's going to give people what they want. He has added French bread pizza, croissants, and brownies to his line of products as well. While other bakery companies are content to stick to a narrow line of products, "I'm bucking the trend," he says. That is, he adds, "if there is a trend." Just as McDonald's expanded its product line and its sales by adding to the hamburger, soft drink, and french fry menu, Liederman thinks that if you have the real estate, you have to offer as much as you can. "I predict the other companies, like Häagen-Dazs and Mrs. Fields and other basically single-product companies, will begin to follow our lead."

Marketing experts may have a lot of profound reasons why David's Cookies sell as well as they do, but Liederman has reduced them all to several simple but rational theories. There is, for example, the Three-Hours-a-Day Theory: "The average American spends three to four hours a day thinking about what they're going to eat, when they're going to eat, or eating. Some spend more.

Me, I spend about twelve." There's also his Cookie-as-Social-Barometer Theory: "Every time the arms race hits the front pages, cookie sales soar because everyone's depressed. We play on human emotions."

But no theory will ever replace the hard work and long hours that are the single common denominator that runs through every successful enterprise, and keeping tabs on his company's seventy direct employees and the 2,000 workers at the various franchises keeps Liederman extremely busy. "The reality is that anybody who runs a business doesn't have the time to do much else other than work," he says. "People who own their own businesses do not check out at five o'clock to go dancing or go to clubs or go out to dinner to unwind or whatever people like that do. We keep on plugging along."

Why does he do it? What drives him to push himself harder, to add to his work load, to expand his responsibilities and his risks? "It's the ultimate dichotomy," he says. "On the one hand, it's a miserable existence, because you always have a gun to your head. On the other hand," he quips, "it beats working. I could close down tomorrow," he admits, "but at this point, for me, the game of what I do is to see what new products I can come out with that people like to eat. And that is very satisfying."

He has contempt for high-priced marketing experts hired by big corporations to conduct market tests for new products. "I think if you have to commission a study and find an outside expert to tell you how to run your business, then you don't understand what your business is in the first place. The main thing about this whole study syndrome is that corporate animals have to cover their rear ends." At his company, he adds, he's never afraid to accept responsibility for a decision — good or bad. People can either take it or leave it, he says, and "most of them stay around because it's more fun to work here. Employees don't have a lot of bureaucracy to contend with, as they do in big corporations. The motto here is just 'get the job done.' "

Children are the one exception to David Liederman's avoidance of outside experts. They are the voices he listens to most. His 4-year-old daughter and her friends often voice opinions about David's macadamia chocolate chunk or the peanut butter chocolate chunk, and they keep up with what's trendy in food through the barrage of advertising that most kids are exposed to every day. Children, he says proudly, are among his products' greatest and most passionate fans. Once, he says, a doctor told him how a child woke up from a coma in a Long Island hospital and his first words were, "Give me a David's cookie." His mother even believes that visions of cookies may have kept the child alive. Feelings as deeply felt as these keep David's Cookies prosperous and growing and ready to take on the world.

It would be a mistake, though, to think that entrepreneurs are only young people like Joel Hyatt or David Liederman, though the majority tend to be relatively young. At the same time, America's growing pool of elderly people have also been among this country's most successful entrepreneurs. For one thing, they often have a lot of extra time on their hands if they're retired; they frequently have unused skills developed and sharpened over a lifetime of work; and very often they have a surplus of energy that just needs to be trained in the right direction. In some sections of the country they have organized their various talents to provide professional consulting to younger businesspeople just getting started who are in need of experienced management advice and counseling. In many cases, they have begun selling a product or service they first began making or providing as a hobby. In other instances, they were forced back into the marketplace by the simple necessity of giving themselves something to do as well as supplementing their income.

Colonel Harland Sanders, the personification of the old Southern gentleman, was retired and living on social security when his friends encouraged him to franchise his secretly seasoned Kentucky fried chicken, which he first began selling at his Corbin, Kentucky, gas station in 1939. An elementary school dropout, Sanders operated a restaurant for twenty-seven years before it failed in 1956 after a nearby highway had been rerouted, sending him into retirement. It wasn't long before he realized that he couldn't get by on social security alone, and he took to the road at the age of 66 to peddle his fried chicken recipe. He sold his franchising enterprise in 1964 to two Kentucky businessmen but retained a position as a salaried "goodwill ambassador," though he became notorious for his undiplomatic comments about the company's food after the firm was sold to Heublein, Inc., in 1971 for $287 million. Sanders died in 1981 at the age of 90, a millionaire, with his fried chicken being sold in 6,000 outlets in all fifty states and more than a dozen countries overseas, dominating the $4.4 billion fast-food chicken market. His name and his face, used on Kentucky Fried's signs and packaging, is one of the most recognized corporate symbols in the world. The colonel's secret recipe, a blend of a dozen different herbs and spices, remains safely stashed away behind eleven locks in a fireproof, bombproof vault at the company's Louisville headquarters.

Or take, for example, some senior citizens tired of sitting on their hands and match them up with homeowners who don't like to leave their homes vacant when they're out of town and you have the makings of a successful business franchise called Home Sitting Services of Denver, Colorado. It was started in 1972 by Al Sutherland, a retired insurance salesman who, after taking care of his son's home and a neighbor's house, thought there was money to be made in a nationwide house-sitting business. Today, there are sixty-five independently owned franchised offices nationwide in such cities as Dallas, Atlanta, Philadelphia, Cleveland, Chicago, Seattle, and San Francisco, as well as the New York, Washington, D.C., and Los Angeles areas. Owners buy the exclusive right to establish a Home Sitting Service for a one-time minimum fee of $6,000 for a city with a population of 100,000. The price goes up in larger localities. "If chicken can have Colonel Sanders," says the soft-spoken but energetic Sutherland, who turned 80 in 1985, "house-sitting can have me." All the house sitters are retirees, with some as "young" as 55. Many work as couples. Barbara Burch, who runs Atlanta's Home Sitting Service, says, "The main reason my sitters do it is to stay involved in the community and feel needed. They get to sit in some of the loveliest homes in Atlanta, giving them a change of pace and scenery. The money is secondary."

Some home sitters feel more like a relative who has come to stay awhile than an employee who receives 37 percent of the $22- to $25-a-day fee charged, a modest supplemental income that doesn't endanger their social security benefits. Popular home sitters get asked back to the same house every time the family goes away, says Joanne Wojahn, the owner of a house-sitting service in Orange County, California. "They enjoy feeling needed, knowing that everything the homeowner might be worried about is getting watched over," she says. In some cases, this includes baby-sitting, pet care, plant watering and even companionship for the older member of the family who stayed home while the others went away. "A lady said she'd probably live ten years longer," as a result of being a house sitter, Sutherland says. Before the woman began her work, "she wasn't interested in life anymore. The biggest problem with retirement is boredom. It's depressing to get up every day and have nothing to do." This is, in fact, much of the appeal for senior citizens who happily work for the house-sitting business.

Besides having someone to care for plants, dogs, or children, the big selling point of Home Sitting Services is crime, because with a home sitter there isn't any. Sutherland says that not a single home watched over by a Home Sitting employee has had a break-in. The business is "a complete winner all around," he adds. It's good for the retirees who want to supplement their income or feel useful and needed. It's good for the people who get someone to look after their homes. And it's good for the owner of the home-sitting business.

The parent company isn't doing too badly either. Today, Home Sitting Services generates around $300,000 a year. Donald J. Foltz, the company's president, who helped Sutherland raise the number of franchise offices from two to sixty-five, says he's "emotionally attached" to the company and has been ever since a banker approached him with the idea of joining it several years ago. He says he can't think of "a better way of earning money than working to keep older Americans employed, active, and happy."

Like Hugh Hefner, who edited and pasted up the galleys for the first edition of *Playboy* magazine on his kitchen table, many entrepreneurs begin their enterprises at home. That was how Tom Phillips started his multimillion-dollar newsletter business in 1974, editing and producing a conservative political newsletter out of his Washington, D.C., apartment, with his wife, Jan, keeping track of subscriptions and renewals, and handling his own direct mail promotion. In his first year, gross sales were $300,000, and he realized that his small newsletter business — providing specialized information to a targeted market — had the potential to become a major communications corporation. Gradually, as his newsletter grew, he began another, then another, in some cases acquiring existing newsletters. His company began to grow rapidly in the 1980s, making the *Inc.* 500 list of fastest-growing privately held businesses in the United States two years in a row, in 1983 and 1984. Today, he employs over one hundred employees and his Potomac, Maryland, company is grossing $12 million a year, publishing more than twenty-five newsletters in the fields of telecommunications, computers, electronic banking, investments, and health. In 1985 he entered the magazine business by acquiring *Mobile Communications Businesses,* a trade journal that specializes in the rapidly growing mobile phone industry. His goal: "To be a major communications organization that will eventually have sales of between $50 million and $100 million a year."

From the very beginning, Phillips says, he "fell in love with newsletters because I thought they were a specialized communications medium in a new age of specialization. People need to know more and more about their own particular fields of specialization, and the newsletter is an excellent vehicle for presenting that type of focused information to small markets." A Dartmouth graduate who majored in government and earned a master's degree in journalism, Phillips has had a love affair with publishing ever since, as a teenager, he took a tour of the *New York Times,* for which his great-aunt was once society editor, and watched "All the news that's fit to print" roll off the huge presses. "I just thought the whole journalism and communications field was exciting, and I wanted to be a part of it." After three years with an advertising agency, and three more with a Washington-based direct mail firm, Phillips was ready to take the plunge on his own, buying his first newsletter from his employer and going into business for himself.

His company has coined the phrase "Actionable information for the '80s," which is the guiding principle behind his newsletters. "We try to give information that can help make a difference in your career or your job or your business or your investments or your health."

The entrepreneurial process both excites and challenges Phillips because the very essence of entrepreneurialism, he believes, is "to create something out of nothing, taking something and visualizing it, bringing it to life. We are living in an entrepreneurial age. Fortunately, in the last decade or so America has awakened to the fact that entrepreneurs have a major contribution to make in creating the businesses of America, founding them, getting them launched, which is a vital role in a dynamic economy. If you don't have continued growth, long term, new business growth, and competition, you end up with a declining or stagnating economy. Now I think there's a new appreciation, all the way from the business schools to the halls of Congress, of the importance of the entrepreneur and small business per se."

What is his advice to entrepreneurs thinking about starting a business of their own? "Have self-confidence, and do it today," he says. "Don't wait for tomorrow. Think things out logically and plan carefully, and once you've got your course set, go full speed ahead. Don't worry about the things that might happen down the road. Plan for contingencies, but don't just sit there thinking of reasons why it won't work. You just need to have enough reasons why it will work and make it work."

In his historic grand tour of America in 1831, Alexis de Tocqueville captured the essence of the American economy when he wrote, "what most astonished me in the United States is not so much the marvelous grandeur of some undertakings as the innumerable multitude of small ones." Today, this unending explosion of inventiveness and creativity and enterprise building is more vibrant and alive than ever before in American history. "Entrepreneurs are once again believed to be the future," says John Sloan, president of the half-million-member National Federation of Independent Business. "Bureaucracies are for the first time believed to be the past." Entrepreneurs, says writer and senior editor Sharon Nelton of *Nation's Business,* "are the stars of the 1980s. Their admiring fans? Venture capitalists, lenders, workers grateful for jobs the entrepreneurs create, and countless people who are dazzled by entrepreneurs' energy, creativity, courage, and zest for what they are doing."

There have been countless American heroes in past eras, people who conquered new frontiers and broke new records and dazzled us and won our hearts with their feats of courage and charismatic ways — from the arenas of politics, space exploration, and the silver screen. Today, however, a new kind of hero has emerged for our times, the entrepreneur, whose national and international appeal offers greater promise for a healthier, happier, and more prosperous society for us all. Yet the journey that entrepreneurs must travel is littered with obstacles, many of which are erected by government, that impede their success and discourage those who would emulate them. It is these obstacles that we will look at next.

Those who view poverty and unemployment as permanent afflictions of our cities fail to understand how rapidly the poor can move up the ladder of success in our economy. But to move up the ladder, they must first get on it.

— *President Ronald Reagan*

You can't create more employees without creating more employers.

— *Congressman Jack Kemp*

CHAPTER 4

Raising the Ladder of Opportunity

ON A BLISTERING HOT DAY in the summer of 1980, Ronald Reagan took his presidential campaign to a rubble-strewn vacant lot in the middle of a South Bronx ghetto and promised to bring economic revitalization to one of the most poverty-stricken communities in America.

Behind him loomed the ghostly ruins of gutted, windowless tenements condemned by local authorities, a scene reminiscent of a bombed-out European city at the conclusion of World War II. The surrounding neighborhood was a wasteland of boarded-up, rat-infested buildings, and closed storefronts. The area was rife with drug abuse, crime, appalling unemployment, and inadequate schools. Reagan's simple proposal to revitalize this and other inner city slums was the enactment of enterprise zones, designated areas where special tax and deregulatory incentives would help nurture business enterprises and job opportunities. The idea had been tried in Great Britain by Prime Minister Margaret Thatcher's government, and with some success.

Reagan's appearance in this New York City slum represented a strategic attack on the failed urban policies of President Jimmy Carter, who had stood on the same spot in his 1976 campaign, promising to help improve the South Bronx's bleak economy with more government assistance programs. Yet despite billions of dollars in Economic Development Administration assistance and Urban Development Action Grants, among countless other government expenditures, little had changed for the better in slums like the South Bronx, Reagan said. In fact, in many respects things had gotten worse, much worse. Nationally, the teenage minority unemployment rate was 27.2 percent in 1964. By 1980 the average jobless rate for black teenagers had officially climbed to 38.5 percent — though many people believed the real jobless rate was much higher than even this. Drug abuse was up sharply among youths and juvenile crime was up too. It was time to try some new ideas, Reagan said, to open up ghetto neighborhoods to free enterprise through proven economic incentives that would stimulate new businesses and help revitalize and expand existing ones.

After he had made his pitch about enterprise zones, a shirt-sleeved Reagan walked across the street to talk with a crowd of largely black and Hispanic residents who stood on an adjoining vacant lot behind some barricades. A crowd of campaign reporters and cameramen pushed and shoved to get close enough to pick up the conversation between the candidate and the South Bronx residents. Perhaps it was the heat of the day, perhaps it was the frustration and cynicism of the area's poor residents, who had heard numerous political promises so many times before, but the meeting between candidate and the crowd soon exploded into an ugly shouting match. They had believed Carter when he promised he would help them, they said, but nothing had changed in their neighborhood or their lives. "So why should we believe you?" some of them yelled. Trying to make himself heard above their shouts and complaints, an exasperated Reagan finally shouted back in an angry tone, "I can't do a damn thing for you unless I get elected."

After assuming the presidency, Reagan made good on at least one part of his promise: he sent legislation to Congress to create enterprise zones for the South Bronx and seventy-four other depressed localities. The bill was promptly introduced by New York congressmen Jack Kemp, a Republican, and Robert Garcia, a Democrat whose district includes the South Bronx. Unfortunately, that poverty-stricken South Bronx neighborhood remains essentially unchanged today, a tragic victim of politics at its worst. Despite more than 258 co-sponsors in the House of Representatives, Reagan's enterprise zones bill has been imprisoned in the Democratic-controlled Ways and Means Committee, where Chairman Dan Rostenkowski of Illinois vowed it would never see the light of day. The liberal Chicago Democrat stubbornly insisted that he opposed the bill only because the U.S. Treasury would lose too much revenue from the measure's modest tax breaks, and thus it would worsen the federal deficit. Of course, Rostenkowski has had no problem backing big Democratic spending bills, which have substantially added to the government's debts. Federal enterprise zones legislation would "cost" an estimated $4 billion to $5 billion in tax expenditures over a five-year period, critics claim,* though it would also eventually yield increased federal tax revenues from new business enterprises and increased employment. The truth of the matter is that at the present time these depressed areas are producing little or no federal tax revenues anyway.

Yet during the summer of 1984, when Reagan was making renewed pleas to House Democratic leaders to free his enterprise zone legislation and let it come up for a vote, the reason behind the Democratic leadership's continued opposition became blatantly clear. For when I asked why Rostenkowski's committee would not send the bill to the House in order to provide some hope of economic relief for seventy-five of the most depressed areas in the country, a top committee official bluntly remarked, "Why should we give Reagan seventy-five media events in the campaign?" To fully appreciate the cynicism and hypocrisy of such opposition to this bill, one need only look at the South Bronx, where more than 40 percent of its residents are below the poverty income line, where overall unemployment hovers around 15 percent, where the youth unemployment rate was over 40 percent at the end of 1985, and where

*The U.S. Treasury estimates that the Kemp-Garcia bill would cost $1.3 billion in lost revenue over three years.

the median family income of $8,448 was the lowest in America. Even more to the point, unemployment and poverty in other inner city ghettos was equally bad.

To its credit, the Senate has passed enterprise zones legislation twice. But there has been no response from the Democratic-controlled House, despite the fact that there is strong support for it among the nation's governors and mayors, many of whom have enacted and implemented their own state and local enterprise zones programs. By 1986, according to the U.S. Department of Housing and Urban Development, five hundred communities in nineteen states had established more than 1,300 enterprise zones, preserving thousands of jobs and creating 50,000 more. Since 1982, these zones have generated more than $2 billion in new investment capital. Ironically, many of the programs have been implemented by Democratic mayors in heavily Democratic communities, including Norwalk, Connecticut; Louisville, Kentucky; Macon, Missouri; and Tampa, Florida. Among the various state and local incentives enacted specifically for these zones: property tax exemptions or reduction; sales tax exemptions or reduction; increased police and fire protection for rundown, crime-ridden areas; streamlined and expedited local regulatory requirements; employer and employee tax credits; investment tax credits; and regulatory relief.

Under the latest version of the proposed federal legislation, one hundred zones would be selected. Communities with high levels of unemployment and poverty would compete for designation by the Department of Housing and Urban Development. Two-thirds of the zones would be in inner cities and one-third would be in rural areas or in small communities. Existing businesses, newly created businesses, or businesses that relocate to such designated zones would receive special investment tax credits for investing in the zone. In addition to receiving exemptions from capital gains taxes, employers would get further tax breaks for hiring disadvantaged workers who reside in the zone and for enlarging their payrolls. And employees would be permitted to take a 5 percent tax credit on their first $10,500 of earned wages. Businesses within the zones could also seek federal regulatory relief from certain government regulations and paperwork requirements, including some export regulations, through their state or local governments.

Among numerous examples of enterprise zones throughout the country, consider these three:

• When the Spiegel mail order company outgrew its Chicago plant, the company considered leaving its trademark city. But the enterprise zone there provided a ground for negotiations: the state and Spiegel worked out a sales and property tax abatement plan that made a $20 million plant renovation possible. The deal helped keep 2,000 jobs in Chicago.

Overall, the city's five zones have helped to stem job losses suffered in the steel industry's decline. During 1984 and 1985, zone incentives were credited with creating 2,000 jobs and saving an additional 5,000. "We're developing several tools to help business expand," says Lynn Cunningham, executive director of the South Chicago Economic Development Commission. "Enterprise zones provide a framework for those tools."

• Suffering an industrial decline similar to that felt in the rustbelt, Louisville, Kentucky, was the first of the state's seven designated zones. That designation gave Louisville 2,145 jobs, both new and retained, as a result of several new small businesses that located in the zone. One-third of those jobs went to those who were unemployed and on welfare. Unique among incentives offered to the Louisville business community was a twenty-year no-strike agreement with labor unions that ensures building construction is completed on schedule.

"Some think that zone tax abatement hurts the city through lost revenue," says Ronald Lewis, chief financial officer at the Huber Corporation in Louisville. "Yet in our first year, as with many businesses, we didn't make any money and didn't pay taxes anyway. But we have a lot of people on our payroll who are off the welfare rolls and now paying taxes."

• Ohio's fifteen designated enterprise zones have been credited with saving and creating more than 12,000 jobs. In Toledo, thirty-five industrial and commercial businesses have settled within zone boundaries, providing 2,500 new jobs. Toledo planners have used zone incentives to promote basic industry, supporting the interdependence of industrial plants and suppliers. "We aim to help labor-intensive industry now fighting foreign competition," says Raymond Boezi, vice-president of Toledo's Seagate Community Development Corporation. "Toledo can't afford to lose big industry. You can't compare a $35,000 a year industrial career with one flipping hamburgers or selling shirts." Among other things, enterprise zone incentives in Toledo helped General Motors complete a $435 million renovation of a stamping plant — saving 1,400 jobs in the area.

The distinguished economist Stuart M. Butler wrote this in his book *Enterprise Zones: Greenlining the Inner Cities:*

> The Enterprise Zone may be the first step toward an escape from the straitjacket we have imposed on our cities. It would create, within the most depressed sections of the inner cities, areas where there would be a conscious attempt to reduce regulation, and to reduce the stifling burden of tax. The zones would be areas where experiments could take place with the minimum of red tape, and where small enterprises could flourish. Not only would these zones bring the innovative power of the small entrepreneur and the neighborhood group to bear on the depressed areas in which they were established, but they would also be laboratories which would provide tested ideas that might have more general application.

Examples of substantial economic growth, urban renovation and construction, and the creation of new jobs and opportunities in areas where there was once nothing but despair and emptiness, show what can be done through market-oriented programs that unleash the power of entrepreneurial initiative. But if entrepreneurs and the free market are to respond vigorously, there must be irresistible incentives, such as lower taxes, more specifically, lower marginal tax rates.

During the 1980 elections, a prominent Democrat said this about the tax-cutting, economic growth policies pursued by President Kennedy in the early 1960s: "At that time, we were able to cut tax rates, increase revenues, add jobs, fund new programs, and keep a stable dollar. That was a good time for a Democrat to be alive. We did a lot of things. One of the reasons was that you could get our nation in a more compassionate frame of mind when you were sharing additional resources from growth. Nobody was losing anything. You could say: 'How about feeding the hungry? How about educating those poor kids? How about having some decent housing for these families that are living in desperate conditions?' People would say, 'That's right. Let's do some of that.'" The speaker, ironically enough, was Walter Mondale, who in 1984 as his party's presidential candidate flatly rejected President Kennedy's economic growth policies, calling instead for tax increases.

Jack Kemp, who loves to quote Mondale on the benefits of the Kennedy tax cuts, says that for once in his life "Walter Mondale got it right." Indeed, says Kemp, "That's what we have tried to do by cutting tax rates across the board. The tax rate cuts were not designed to be an attack on government or its revenues. They were an effort to get the country moving again. We need a safety net, but we also need a ladder of opportunity. And opportunities on the public payroll are not a substitute for jobs in the private sector."

In many ways and in many parts of our country, the bottom rungs of that ladder of opportunity have been cut out, as we shall examine in the next couple of chapters. For decades the politicians in Washington have misguidedly sought to replace the broken rungs of the ladder with a plethora of federal grants, loans, and loan guarantee programs for a select list of economic straphangers who know how to fill out the multitude of federal forms and applications in order to get on board the gravy train. But such programs as the Economic Development Administration (EDA), the Small Business Administration (SBA), and Urban Development Action Grants (UDAG), among many others, have touched only a tiny fraction of people and communities, and very often have redistributed funds to those least in need.

Out of the total of 14.3 million small businesses, a minuscule 0.2 percent have received subsidized SBA credit. Of all new small businesses created each year, fewer than 1 percent are helped by SBA. So whom are SBA's loan guarantees helping? Certainly not people struggling to get on the bottom rungs of the economic ladder. On the contrary, according to the Office of Management and Budget, between 1981 and 1982 loan guarantees totaling $143 million went to doctors, dentists, and veterinarians — professionals who are in the upper-income category, are generally good credit risks, and who are thus unworthy of SBA handouts.

Similarly, out of the $440 million a year being distributed in Urban Development Action Grants to assist corporate interests, a mere twenty big cities have scooped up 44 percent of all UDAG dollars and 34 percent of all projects. Moreover, pork barrel programs like EDA, SBA, UDAG, and so forth were redistributing tens of billions of dollars — money that had to be removed from the economy in the first place through higher taxation — largely on the basis of political criteria, not on the basis of wise and productive investments in the economy. Former budget director David Stockman says that during the 1980 presidential campaign, the Carter administration used the $440 million-a-year UDAG program "as the biggest election boondoggle in history. They put out UDAG grants all over the country in 1980," he says, to assist Carter's reelection efforts. The argument is made that a UDAG stimulates new private investment and increases jobs, but in truth, says Stockman, it simply "moves it from one city to another. It doesn't do anything. It just stirs around the pot." No net new jobs are created, because the money taken from an area through taxation means that area loses productive, job-creating funds it would have spent on business projects chosen for their merit as sound investments, not for political considerations.

Even the late Senator Robert F. Kennedy of New York, who enthusiastically applauded the establishment of many of these programs under the Johnson administration in the 1960s, came to realize their fundamental flaw — that the war on poverty sought only government solutions, to the exclusion and the diminishment of the private sector. "By failing to involve the private sector," Kennedy observed in the late 1960s, "we have not only ignored the potential contribution of millions of talented and energetic Americans in thousands of productive enterprises. More dangerously, we have created for the poor a separate economy, a second-rate system of government agencies keeping the poor apart from the rest of us."

In place of the government's costly pork barrel acronyms, which have done little or nothing to rescue and rebuild America's most depressed localities, the need in the 1980s is to restore the broken rungs on the ladder of opportunity and to unleash the power of economic growth. We must do that by reducing taxes further, especially among lower-income families and among businesses just getting started. America will not become stronger economically by taxing its citizens and businesses more, or by trying to make the rich poorer. America will continue to grow and prosper only by strengthening and broadening the system of economic incentives that enable the poor to become rich. It is of the utmost importance to constantly strive to improve opportunities for all people to enter the economic mainstream and move up the income scale as rapidly as their ambition and determination will take them. Further reducing taxation at the local, state, and federal level, and making access to the marketplace easier through increased deregulation at all levels of government, is the best way to make America truly an opportunity society.

But if we are to further reduce tax rates, we must of necessity find new and sophisticated approaches to restrain the growth in government spending. Businessman Peter Grace, a lifelong Democrat and the feisty chief executive officer of W. R. Grace & Company who headed President Reagan's Private Sector Survey on Cost Control, once told me that he wasn't surprised at the level of waste and mismanagement he discovered in the federal bureaucracy. What did surprise him, Grace said, was "the extraordinary degree to which the president's hands are tied" in managing the money Congress gives him to run the government. Micromanaging many federal programs right down to, in some cases, deciding who is going to get the grants and whether certain federal field offices can be closed, Congress has filled its appropriations and authorization bills with a raft of provisos, prohibitions, and directives that tell the president's departmental and agency chiefs what they can and cannot do in terms of managing their programs.

The Grace Commission made 2,478 management and policy recommendations that would save taxpayers $424.4 billion over three years. Most of the big ticket recommendations require legislative action that, unfortunately, has not been forthcoming from Congress. The Pentagon, for example, wants to close some fifty outdated and inefficient military facilities that it no longer needs to operate, at a potential savings of $2 billion. But Congress forbids it. Amtrak, the national rail passenger service, wants to close rail lines on which ridership is very poor. But Congress forbids it. The Agriculture Department wants to cease funding many of the extension service programs that are located in counties where there are few if any farmers. But Congress forbids it.

Congress must give the chief executive, through his departmental and agency managers, a freer rein to seek more competitive bidding on government procurement, a wider latitude to close or curtail unneeded bureaucracies, and more independence to make other prudent but innovative economies to lower the government's operating and management costs. The Grace Commission estimates this could save billions of dollars annually.

Meantime, federal spending has been growing at a furious pace, slowing the rate of growth the U.S. economy could be experiencing if wasteful spending were significantly reduced. According to the Office of Management and Budget, federal spending in 1985 leaped upward by more than $100 billion in the space of a single year. Think of it, a single year. Federal outlays sprang from $841.8 billion in fiscal 1984 to an estimated $946.6 billion in fiscal 1985. Yearly federal spending was expected to exceed $1 trillion by the end of 1986 for the first time in U.S. history. These numbers have been pushed upward by a raft of unneeded pork barrel and special interest spending that could be held down if the president were given the management tools to do the job. One of the most important tools that we can give the president is the line-item veto, which would allow him with the stroke of a pen to prune billions from the federal budget. Forty-three governors use the line-item veto authority to cut billions from their budgets, thereby keeping them in balance with revenues. But the nation's chief executive possesses no such power.

There was a time when the regular veto was sufficient to deal with relatively small appropriations bills whose rejection and delay would in no way harm the workings of government. But that is no longer the case in an era of megabudget bills, which can contain hundreds of billions of dollars in a single appropriations measure, affecting hundreds of agencies and programs. If the president is strongly opposed to spending provisions in a funding bill, he has only two distasteful choices under the Constitution: he can veto the entire bill, or he can approve the additional spending and drive taxpayers deeper into debt. "The full veto worked fine in a bygone era when budget bills were relatively small and dealt with only a few programs," says Senator Mack Mattingly of Georgia. "But nowadays the President needs a modern precision tool to trim the fat."

This "like it or lump it" choice faced President Reagan in October 1984, when Congress tossed a $458 billion appropriations bill on his desk, the largest appropriations package in American history. The bill funded everything from the Defense Department to vital health and welfare programs, but it also was packed with hundreds of wasteful and unnecessary expenditures that cried out for a presidential veto: among them, $400,000 to study the 1932–33 famine in the Ukraine and $2 million to reconstruct the Nantucket, Massachusetts, lighthouse "in its original form." The president had little choice but to sign. A full veto might have shut down vital programs for weeks until Congress hammered out a new bill.

On the other hand, if the president had line-item veto power — under which Congress would have full authority to override his actions — he could erase the wasteful and low-priority items he opposed, quickly bringing spending into line with federal revenues, and then sign the bill into law. The line-item veto is not a substitute for congressional and executive branch restraint in spending, but it is a useful tool that would help a president to rein in uncontrolled federal spending. Economic growth, increased capital investment, expanded exports, and lower interest rates are all tied inextricably to a reduction in federal spending. Every dollar that is not taxed and spent by Washington is another dollar that will be saved, invested, or spent by business or consumers, nourishing greater economic growth and helping to raise the ladder of opportunity for all Americans.

The greatest enemy of the entrepreneur is government intervention.

— *Professor Perry Gresham*
BETHANY COLLEGE

Cutting back the size and burden of regulation would enable the private enterprise system once again to become the central engine of economic progress in our nation.

— *Professor Murray L. Weidenbaum*
THE FUTURE OF BUSINESS REGULATION

CHAPTER 5

Obstacles to Growth

FOR TWENTY-FIVE YEARS, Allan B. Robbins, a feisty, hardworking, independent truck driver from Monson, Massachusetts, trucked across America in open violation of the costly, anticompetitive transportation laws policed by the government.

Robbins really wasn't doing anything that most Americans would consider illegal. He was simply trying to make a decent living for his family by hauling construction equipment around the country — but without the official sanction of the Interstate Commerce Commission, the nation's oldest federal regulatory agency, or fulfilling the excessive record-keeping demands of the U.S. Department of Transportation. "I hate paperwork," he says. Yet Allan Robbins's story is more than just a tale of a 61-year-old small businessman who was the object of repeated government harassment, penalties, and counterproductive regulations. It is also the little-told story about how government in a thousand and one ways, both big and small, inhibits business growth, throttles job creation, and sometimes treats honest, hardworking Americans like outlaws.

The government's persecution cost him more than $50,000 in fines, legal fees, and other expenses; but the real costs ran much deeper, not only for Robbins but for businesses like his throughout the country. Were it not for the government's chilling intrusion, "I would have a business twice as big as I have now," he says regretfully. Multiply Allan Robbins's experience by a thousand small businesspeople like him, by a hundred thousand, by a million, and one quickly understands the awesome cost of government regulation to the economy.

Robbins has been trucking ever since he started hauling lime for farmers as a boy of 15 in western Massachusetts. After serving with distinction in World War II as a B-29 commander, he returned home, bought a rig, and started in the heavy hauling business. Today, he has a dozen vehicles and employs six people, including his daughter, who is the company bookkeeper, and his two sons, who drive full-time.

Years ago, however, he decided that it just wasn't worth the substantial effort and cost to secure an ICC interstate license. So, he did what he knew "hundreds of other truckers are doing" — he ignored the federal regulations and kept right on trucking. "They [ICC authorities] got me in 1960 and they've been on me ever since," he once said, as if he were talking about the secret police. He tried to buy out another trucking firm several years ago, along with the certificate and routes that went with it, but the ICC wouldn't allow it. The bigger trucking firms in the area didn't want the competition and vehemently protested.

The government was relentless in its persecution, but Robbins was just as determined that he had a God-given right to drive his truck and carry goods, free of federal interference. Over a thirteen-year period alone, Robbins shelled out more than $9,000 in fines to the government, and the Department of Transportation charged him on numerous occasions with failing to keep federally required safety and medical records. It forced him to be scrupulously careful about avoiding detection by government agents, taking circuitous routes and back roads, which resulted in a lot of wasteful return trips with an empty truck. All of this cost him dearly in time, energy, and precious capital. And the government didn't like it one bit.

Yet whom was he really hurting? This rarely asked question was posed when Robbins was finally hauled up before an ICC administrative law judge in 1984. After listening to three days of argument by Robbins's attorney and federal prosecutors, Judge Nolin J. Bilodeau surprised everyone by admitting that Robbins's failure to comply with the federal trucking bureaucracy hadn't really hurt anyone. On the contrary, the ICC judge found that Robbins — whom he gently called "an independent soul" — had faithfully provided excellent service to his customers and that his highway safety record was "exemplary."

In an unexpected and breathtaking decision that shook federal regulators to their roots, Bilodeau ruled that instead of punishing Robbins, "consideration should be given to the man's strong feeling that he had a constitutional right to operate unimpeded by governmental red tape." While expressing the hope that Robbins eventually will have "a change in attitude" toward government regulations, the judge granted him a fifteen-month operating certificate. But, ignoring Ronald Reagan's's pledge to "get the government off our backs," the ICC — an independent regulatory agency set apart by Congress from the executive branch — and the Department of Transportation appealed Bilodeau's ruling. The matter went before the full commission, which eventually ruled in Robbins's favor.

The ICC is a tiny and somewhat obscure federal agency, but its requirements that truck, bus, limousine, and other surface transportation entrepreneurs must first obtain a license from the government, and meet a host of regulatory requirements, before entering the marketplace has had a chilling effect on this important sector of the economy. Though deregulation of the ICC in recent years has opened up what used to be a closed industry that permitted few new entrants, the continued existence of this agency, with all its attendant regulations and paperwork, has kept thousands of small entrepreneurs from entering the transportation business and thousands more from expanding existing operations. Greater economic growth derives in large part from easy access to the marketplace, allowing any and all entrepreneurs the freedom to begin any legally permissible business they choose. The degree to which government blocks access to the marketplace reduces in equal measure the potential for new business formation and job creation. Tragically, lower-income persons, largely members of minority groups, have been hurt most by such senseless regulation. For example, the trucking, limousine, and delivery businesses require a relatively small initial investment and thus are among the easiest businesses for unskilled, undereducated workers to enter. And, within a free market, if they work hard enough, they'll grow and prosper.

Allan Robbins fervently believes that anyone who wants to haul goods for profit in interstate commerce should be free to do so, unencumbered by the government. "I was born with that birthright," he insists. "If a guy's got a truck, he should be allowed to run freight just the way I do." Sadly, this remains a radical idea in today's still-overregulated economy.

Throughout her relatively short but distinguished career in Congress, Texas Democrat Barbara Jordan was an untiring voice of compassion for the poor. But she, along with many of her colleagues, was also a builder and/or supporter of numerous obstacles to expanding the job market for the very people for whom she professed so much compassion. I will never forget the day I interviewed the congresswoman in her Capitol Hill office in 1977, shortly after the House of Representatives had killed a youth minimum wage differential bill that would have put thousands of America's poor, unskilled youths to work. The issue had been fought out before in Congress, only to lose to organized labor, which has long been bitterly opposed to a lower minimum wage for young people. This time, though, northern moderates and some liberals were spearheading the push for the lower minimum, arguing that youth unemployment had become intolerably high, especially among minorities in the inner cities and poor rural areas. The key vote occurred on an amendment offered by Representative Robert J. Cornell, Democrat of Wisconsin, which would have allowed employers to pay workers aged 18 and younger 85 percent of the mandatory minimum wage during their first six months on the job.

In talking with me, the articulate Jordan, who returned to private life at the end of 1980, seemed uneasy and frustrated about the vote she had cast that afternoon. Wearily leaning back in her black leather chair, Jordan confessed, "I came very close to voting for that proposal. We've got to do something about high unemployment among our youth." Tragically, despite the shocking national, regional, and area jobless statistics that existed then, as they exist now, Barbara Jordan had voted against any deviation from organized labor's sacred minimum wage law — even though America's black youths suffer more than any other minority from chronic unemployment.

She had every reason to feel uncomfortable about her vote, because she would have made the difference between victory or defeat. The Democratic-controlled House killed the minimum wage bill, 210–211, by a one-vote tie-breaker cast by Speaker Thomas P. "Tip" O'Neill of Massachusetts. A switch in her vote would not only have assured passage of the amendment, but also could well have encouraged others to follow her leadership. It was a leadership that was sorely lacking in the House and one that was sorely needed. At the time the roll call vote was taken, the unemployment rate among all blacks and other minorities in O'Neill's hometown of Boston was nearly 14 percent, and among minority youths it was double that amount. In Jordan's hometown of Houston the jobless rate among black youths was an incredible 25 percent. Nationally at that time, the jobless rate among black youths was a staggering 41.1 percent. Yet on that day, O'Neill, Jordan, and 209 of their House colleagues sent America's's jobless youths this message: "Sorry, but it's better that you remain on the streets and unemployed rather than have the opportunity to work for something less than the minimum wage, develop good work habits, and get on the first rung of the economic ladder."

Overall, young people make up nearly one-third of the nation's jobless. While total unemployment was running 6.9 percent nationally at the end of 1985, it was 18.9 percent among the 16-to-19-year-old age group. Far worse, black youth unemployment stood at 42.7 percent at the end of 1984. Even though unemployment rates fell overall as a result of the economic recovery throughout 1983, 1984, and 1985, the rates for unemployed youths still remained brutally high in many areas of the country. In Washington, D.C., the black youth jobless rate in 1984 was 40.5 percent, and 36.5 percent for all 16-to-19-year-old youths in the nation's capital. Elsewhere, black youth unemployment was nearly 53 percent in Chicago, and overall youth unemployment was 30 percent in New York City and 25 percent in Philadelphia. In Los Angeles the jobless rate among young blacks was nearly 40 percent, 30 percent among Hispanic youths, and 23.5 percent among all youths. In Newark, black youth joblessness was running 45 percent.

Persistently high youth unemployment has been a festering social wound in America, resulting in empty, wasted lives and contributing to increased drug abuse, teenage pregnancies, poverty, and crime. The chief cause? There are a number of factors — from poor public education programs to low rates of economic growth in local economies. But a major factor is the inflexible hourly minimum wage law, which prevents unemployed, unskilled, and severely undereducated minority youths from being absorbed into America's economic mainstream. The rigid minimum wage has cruelly priced these people out of the labor market. Yet Congress stubbornly refuses to enact even a modest youth differential, blindly swallowing the AFL-CIO's cant that it will result in young workers pushing older workers out of their jobs. In point of fact, however, few employers are going to replace experienced, productive employees with unskilled workers whose productivity does not match or exceed their pay. Besides, the Reagan administration's Youth Employment Opportunity Wage proposal would specifically forbid such practices. "For the most part," says economist Walter Williams of George Mason University, "teenagers hired at the subminimum rate would fill new jobs or old jobs that would be reinstated. There might be ushers at movies again, for example, and hotels might decide to keep their corridors and windows cleaner." Many other entry-level jobs that have been eliminated through cost-cutting moves such as self-service gas pumps and salad bars in restaurants may also be restored.

Numerous studies have clearly revealed the insidious effect the minimum wage has had on job creation in general. A 1983 report from the General Accounting Office (GAO), Congress's chief investigating and auditing arm, concluded that not only does the minimum wage reduce the availability of jobs nationally, but the number of low-skilled, entry-level jobs has declined as the minimum wage has increased: *"GAO found virtually total agreement that employment is lower than it would have been if no minimum wage existed, even during periods of substantial employment growth."* (Emphasis added.)

In 1981 a congressionally created Minimum Wage Study Commission discovered that when the official minimum wage rises, youth employment goes down. The commission, which Congress instructed to review the social, political, and economic consequences of the minimum wage, said that cutting the $3.35 per hour minimum to $2.50 per hour for teenagers would have produced up to 356,000 new jobs. Yet in spite of this significant finding, the commission ended up rejecting the idea of a youth wage differential, causing one of its members, S. Warne Robinson, to charge angrily that the commission had totally disregarded the facts. Said Robinson: "The Commission majority's near-total disregard for facts became apparent as the results of our economic research began taking shape. With the overwhelming bulk of the evidence from these studies showing that the minimum wage hurts far more poor families than it helps, the majority proclaimed the view that Congress did not really expect the Commission to base its recommendations on the facts anyway. When the evidence became inescapable that a rising minimum wage wipes out millions of job opportunities for young people, women, the elderly and the disadvantaged, the commission's majority did not even bother to refute the facts. They were simply declared immaterial."

Ronald Reagan has long been critical of the obstacles the minimum wage creates against opening up job opportunities for those on the lowest rung of the economic ladder. Indeed, during his 1980 presidential campaign Reagan declared, "The minimum wage has caused more misery and unemployment than anything since the Great Depression." Yet when Senator Orrin Hatch of Utah, chairman of the Senate Labor and Human Resources Committee, held hearings in 1981, the administration inexplicably refused to take any position on legislation to allow a lower minimum for youths seeking work. By 1983, however, the president was aggressively proposing a $2.50 minimum Youth Opportunity Wage for workers up to the age of 21, solely during the summer months. Others, such as then-senator Charles Percy of Illinois, were urging a $2.85 youth minimum under similar restrictions, while Senator Don Nickles of Oklahoma wanted flatly to exempt anyone under age 18 from the minimum wage law.

But these proposals have gotten nowhere in Congress as a result of organized labor's hold on key lawmakers and committees. Hatch, for example, has been powerless to get them through his own Labor committee, even though Republicans are in the majority. The reason: the panel's two liberal Republican mavericks, Senator Robert Stafford of Vermont and Senator Lowell Weicker, Jr., of Connecticut, are in league with the committee's Democrats in opposition to this important job-creating reform. Meantime, a huge wall of opposition to minimum wage reform also exists in the House, where Democratic leaders remain firmly opposed to any change.

Nevertheless, a few hairline cracks are beginning to appear in this government-built barrier to job creation, and they seem to be growing larger. In a surprising break with its traditional allies — the Congressional Black Caucus, the Urban League, the National Association for the Advancement of Colored People, and organized labor — the National Conference of Black Mayors, which represents 253 cities, came out four square for a minimum wage youth differential in 1984. The black mayors, who must deal with the grim reality of high youth unemployment in their inner city neighborhoods, and the tragic by-products of unemployment, crime, and drug abuse, believe every incentive ought to be pursued to nourish job creation.

"As mayors, being in the trenches, so to speak, we are confronted almost daily with young people in and out of our city halls pleading for jobs," says Mayor Walter Tucker of Compton, California. "Something must be done to begin to turn around the high unemployment rate among our young people," adds Mayor Johnny

Ford of Tuskegee, Alabama, the former president of the National Conference of Black Mayors. "We've got to get the young people off the [street] corners and into meaningful job opportunities." Similarly, Mayor Marion Barry of Washington, D.C., complains, "We have thousands of young people out of work. I'd rather be criticized for supporting the Youth Employment Opportunity Act at $2.50 and save the $15,000 it costs to keep [a wayward youth] incarcerated" for a year. As for his black brothers in Congress who consider Barry's words tantamount to treason, Barry replies, "Those who are against this all have jobs — none of them are beating the pavement trying to find work."

Apparently, the black mayors have considerable black support among the public for their position. A nationwide survey by Data Black Public Opinion Polls found that nearly 40 percent of blacks surveyed supported a subminimum wage to put black teenagers to work. Department of Labor economists believe that a youth subminimum would create from 450,000 to 600,000 jobs for young people. "We cannot afford to wait any longer," says Dewey Thomas, Jr., of the National Association of Minority Contractors. "We must provide youth with a 'first step' into the world of work, a step that will foster the development of job skills and work habits that will assist them in future career development." Sadly, however, the prospects for congressional reform on this vital social and economic issue remain as bleak as the chances of a poor, uneducated, unskilled, inner city 17-year-old black youth finding his first job at $3.35 an hour.

Yet there are other government-created obstacles to earning a living that strike even closer to home. In fact, they actually forbid earning a living at home in a number of occupations. This, despite the fact that Labor Department studies project that within the next fifteen years as many as 15 million people will be working in their homes. Much of this growth will be due to the increased use of computers and computer communications in service-connected industries; but a lot of it, too, will involve the increased production of various crafts and services at home. Presently, the Census Bureau says 5 million people work and earn a living at home; but that is based on 1980 data, and the figure today is believed to be much higher. The reason: a multitude of cottage industries have grown up in recent years, making it possible for poor, abandoned, or divorced women to support their young children at home and stay off welfare; for the elderly and the handicapped to supplement inadequate fixed incomes; and for low-income families to make ends meet and be self-sufficient. But Labor Department regulations have not only stymied such efforts to succeed in the homeworker marketplace, they have prohibited their expansion and growth.

The issue of the government versus the home entrepreneur was raised in 1979 when U.S. Labor Department agents from the Boston regional office trooped through the snows of Vermont to uncover a bunch of women who were knitting sweaters, ski hats, and scarves in their homes. Worse, the agents discovered, the women were selling the items for profit! The department, then being run by Jimmy Carter's secretary of labor, Ray Marshall, denounced the home knitters, saying they were violating some obscure regulations under the Fair Labor Standards Act. The regulations prohibit the manufacture of seven products by homeworkers, all of which compete with union-dominated industries, including knitted outerwear. An editorial cartoon in Vermont's *Rutland Herald* ridiculed the Labor Department's action by portraying federal agents crouched behind their cars outside a snow-covered cottage as a burly government agent shouted through a bullhorn at a frightened elderly woman inside who was peeking through her window, "Throw out your knitting needles and come out with your hands up!"

The controversy further escalated when the Reagan administration came into office in 1981 and Labor Secretary Raymond Donovan, after receiving more than 10,000 complaints and holding public hearings, abolished the homeworker rule for knitters. The International Ladies Garment Workers Union (ILGWU), which originally engineered the regulations back in the 1940s to eliminate any competition from nonunion homeworkers, immediately took the case to court. The ILGWU's general counsel, Max Zinny, remarked at the time that home knitters "should find some other way to occupy themselves." But after a lengthy legal battle, with numerous and costly twists and turns, the knitters eventually won.

There are an estimated 60,000 home knitters around the country, people like Mrs. Virginia Gray, who, with her husband, Roland, a retired farmer, lives in a little cottage in the green hills of Greensboro, Vermont, on his social security benefits of $400 a month. The gentle but industrious Mrs. Gray, 66, knits more than eight hundred handsome ski sweaters in a single year, clearing in one year more than $12,000 after taxes. Her handiwork is purchased by David Putnam, an innovative entrepreneur whose company, Vermont Woolens, Ltd., of Stowe, sells the merchandise to stores around the country. He thus provides work for dozens of women, most of whom would be unable to leave their homes to find employment. "We've got everything from young mothers with kids at home to farmers' wives with cows at home to older women who don't want to stand at a checkout counter all day," says Putnam.

Other entrepreneurs are running similar cottage industry businesses by purchasing the work of women who wish to stay at home but remain financially independent. In many cases, these women have branched out to run their own businesses. Audrey Pudvah is a typical example of a woman who has since gone into business for herself. She has built a knitting room onto her log cabin home in East Calais, Vermont, and is turning out Audrey's Designs.

The point is simply this: there is something morally wrong with government economic policy when Americans who want nothing more than the freedom to work for themselves must travel to Washington to plead for that right. *Chicago Tribune* columnist Joan Beck thought the ban against the knitters was particularly unconscionable because it interfered "with women's freedom to work where and when they choose," preventing them from making their occupation "more compatible with family life and child rearing."

But the knitting regulation was only a tiny part of an ocean of government obstacles to expanding economic opportunities for all Americans. Remaining on the Department of Labor's list of prohibited homeworker cottage industries are the manufacture of jewelry, gloves, buttons, buckles, handkerchiefs, embroideries, and women's apparel — occupations that have been traditionally pursued by low- to moderate-income people because the primary investment to beginning such a business is one's labor and skills. Yet as harmful and counterproductive as these regulations are in and of themselves, their effect is even more destructive in that they discourage individual initiative and creativity in related occupational fields simply by their very existence. "The feminization of poverty is not going to be arrested while the federal government makes it hard for women to earn money," says National Public Radio commentator Connie Marshner. "These antiquated regulations should be eliminated." For now and the foreseeable future, however, anyone beginning a home enterprise in these prohibited occupations still risks reprisals from Big Brother in Washington.

Few industries have experienced such rapid growth as has the package delivery service, creating hundreds of thousands of new private sector jobs. United Parcel Service now carries up to 70 percent of all parcels. And companies like Federal Express, which revolutionized mail delivery with its overnight delivery service, has spawned numerous competitors. The federally subsidized U.S. Postal Service responded with its Express Mail service. But it frequently fails to deliver on its 3:00 P.M. next day guarantee, while commercial competitors like Federal Express are delivering letters and packages by 10:30 A.M.

These private delivery firms have not only created new jobs on their payrolls but have spawned subcontractors and additional employment in related service industries. Yet far more jobs could be added to the letter and package delivery industry if the government would simply repeal the Postal Service's monopoly over first-class mail. In recent years, many have tried to enter the postal business, offering to deliver first-class mail cheaper, faster, and more reliably, only to have the government haul them into court and threaten them with fines and imprisonment if they persisted. An Oklahoma entrepreneur was blocked by federal prosecutors from delivering mail in 1971. Ten-year-old Cub Scouts in New York, who were trying to raise money delivering Christmas cards, were threatened with a $76,500 fine in 1976. A Rochester, New York, firm offering same-day delivery for ten cents a letter was stopped cold in federal court in 1978. The *New York Times* remarked at the time that it wished the Postal Service was as fast as its lawyers. (The stubborn persistence with which the government holds on to its postal monopoly is illustrated by the fact that even in Great Britain, where the government runs everything from an automobile company to a broadcasting business, the postal service allows private delivery of Christmas cards.)

While most Americans realize this, it bears repeating: first-class U.S. mail service has deteriorated badly and is now about 10 percent slower than it was fifteen years ago. On the average, it takes a day and a half to deliver a letter — even three days is deemed acceptable according to Postal Service standards — which is somewhat slower than it was in 1969. Moreover, since 1970 the cost of a first-class stamp has gone up seven times. Postal workers unions have pushed the average pay-plus-benefits for postal employees to more than $24,000 a year. Postal subsidies approached $1 billion a year in 1985 — money taken out of a productive private sector to support certain classes of mail as well as to make up for inefficiency and mismanagement in an operation the government has no business running.

It is difficult to say how many new businesses and jobs would be created by ending the government's monopoly on first-class mail. Certainly it would be in the hundreds of thousands. One need only let one's entrepreneurial imagination take flight to conjure up the myriad commercial possibilities for mail deliveries of all types — overnight, electronic, and regular — to envision the countless enterprises and job opportunities that would result. For the foreseeable future, however, the government's needless and senseless postal monopoly will prevent these opportunities from being realized.

From the foregoing examples, it should be clear that the most robust growth rate among new businesses in recent years has been in deregulated industries. Even during 1981 and 1982, the deepest trough of the Great Recession, new businesses in the communications, financial services, and transportation industries — all of which have been significantly deregulated — increased by 24.8 percent, more than twice the 11.1 percent rate of increase in the overall economy. Though business creations decreased overall by 0.1 percent annually between 1980 and 1982, new local and urban transportation businesses increased by nearly 17 percent, new banking firms by 69 percent, and new transportation service firms by 11 percent, according to Dun & Bradstreet Corporation.

Most of this growth stemmed from deregulation begun by Congress in the mid-to-late 1970s and the early 1980s in such regulatory agencies as the Federal Communications Commission, the Interstate Commerce Commission, and the Civil Aeronautics Board, which was dismantled. The Airline Deregulation Act of 1978 allowed airlines to select or abandon any routes they chose, to enter new markets, and to raise or lower their rates at will. The Bus Regulatory Reform Act of 1982 freed bus companies from having to apply to the ICC for operating authority. The Motor Carrier Act of 1980 significantly deregulated the trucking industry, opening up greater access to the interstate transportation markets. The Thrift Institutions Restructuring Act of 1982 allowed savings and loans to issue loans of up to 10 percent of their assets and permitted investments in small business investment companies and nonresidential personal property. The Staggers Rail Act of 1980 significantly reduced the authority of the ICC over railroad rates and opened up the industry to price competition. The Depository Institutions Deregulation and Monetary Control Act of 1980 allowed mutual savings banks to issue business, corporate, and commercial loans of up to 5 percent of their assets, removed interest rate ceilings, and allowed payment of interest on demand deposits.

All of this has dramatically stimulated new business start-ups, providing further proof of the degree to which deregulation has contributed to economic growth, especially in the area of small businesses. According to President Reagan's 1985 report to Congress *The State of Small Business:*

> The deregulation of certain sectors of the U.S. economy has resulted in sizable benefits for small businesses. New products have been introduced and new markets have opened in formerly regulated industries. Prices have fallen, and thousands of new firms and new jobs have been created. Small firms with fewer than 100 employees have contributed a disproportionate percentage of new jobs in deregulated industries — from 52 percent in 1976–1982 to 83 percent in 1980–1982.
>
> Deregulation has affected both sides of the economic equation. Many new small firms have begun supplying newly competitive

> markets in the deregulated sectors; business customers — both large and small — have been affected by price reductions and service innovations in these sectors.

Nevertheless, the layers of government regulation run very deep, and many barriers to increased business formation and job creation still remain, even in agencies where significant deregulation has already taken place. Trucking entrepreneurs should not have to apply to Washington for a permit in order to truck goods across state lines. Railroads should not have to clear their economic decision making — route eliminations or rate increases — with a federal agency. Women working at home should not have to fear that they may be violating federal law if they create a product for sale in interstate markets. Entrepreneurs should be free to offer the delivery of first-class mail to anyone they choose for any rate they choose. The sooner these and many other remaining obstacles are eliminated, the sooner expanded economic opportunities are going to become available in every corner of the land — especially to those Americans for whom the promise of America is still a distant dream.

How is it moral to put one group of citizens out of work, for reasons they do not understand, in favor of another? How is it moral for government to deceive its constituents by telling them that it is "creating" jobs, when it knows in fact that it is not?

— *Professor Thomas J. DiLorenzo*
GEORGE MASON UNIVERSITY

CHAPTER 6

Creating Jobs

IT IS CALLED America's economic miracle and it is the envy of the world. Yet most of the world's nations still haven't figured out how we do it. It is what continues to bring waves of immigrants to our shores and across our borders — over half a million a year (570,000 in 1985) from every corner of the globe, more than 5 million people in the last decade alone — seeking opportunity and the promise of a better life. It is a phenomenon that arises out of the inextinguishable spirit of enterprise that beats within the heart of the American economy. America's economic miracle is its extraordinary ability to create jobs.

By the end of 1985, the U.S. unemployment rate had fallen to 6.9 percent. Ten million more people were employed between November 1982 and April 1986, a fact that stunned critics of supply-side economics and opponents of Ronald Reagan's tax cuts and caused some nations around the world, even socialist India, to begin cutting their taxes and reducing economic regulations in the hope of emulating us. With the U.S. work force numbering 110 million, we are employing the highest percentage of our population in his-

Table 1
JOBS CREATED BETWEEN 1961 AND 1985

Year to Year	Number of Jobs Lost or Gained*
1960–61	7,000 gained
1961–62	1,117,000 gained
1962–63	1,005,000 gained
1963–64	1,555,000 gained
1964–65	1,711,000 gained
1965–66	1,983,000 gained
1966–67	1,573,000 gained
1967–68	1,583,000 gained
1968–69	1,967,000 gained
1969–70	656,000 gained
1970–71	544,000 gained
1971–72	2,626,000 gained
1972–73	2,872,000 gained
1973–74	1,677,000 gained
1974–75	991,000 lost
1975–76	2,896,000 gained
1976–77	3,253,000 gained
1977–78	4,006,000 gained
1978–79	2,742,000 gained
1979–80	486,000 gained
1980–81	1,135,000 gained
1981–82	848,000 lost
1982–83	1,316,000 gained
1983–84	4,192,000 gained
1984–85	2,154,000 gained

Source: The U.S. Bureau of Labor Statistics' Current Population Survey, from *Employment and Earnings,* Vol. 33, No. 4, April 1986.

Note: If employment growth is measured from November 1982 (the economy's low point during the 1981–82 recession) through April 1986, the U.S. Bureau of Labor Statistics shows an increase of 10 million in the nation's employment rolls during this period.

tory. To put our job-producing machine into even sharper perspective, we need only to look at Europe, where by mid-1985 the average jobless rate was about 15 percent and where anemic economies have lost almost 2 million jobs since 1980. Even the superindustrious Japanese have been unable to match the more than 10 million new jobs created in the United States during this period. Between 1970 and 1984, Japan's employment rolls increased by 6 million people, an 11.7 percent increase, compared to more than 29 million new jobs created in the United States, a breathtaking 36 percent increase. Over a one-year period between 1984 and 1985, the U.S. economy produced more than 2 million new jobs while Japan created only 400,000.

Nevertheless, 8 million Americans remained out of work at the end of 1985, and pockets of deep unemployment persisted in many areas of the country, especially in America's depressed rural areas and decaying inner cities.

But none of this has to be. The answer is to stimulate higher rates of economic growth and more business formation — especially in areas where unemployment is highest. The challenge for America is to find ways to unleash the limitless productive energies of its marketplace and thus produce more enterprises and more employment opportunities for anyone seeking a job and a better standard of living.

It should be no secret that economic growth is highest and unemployment lowest in those areas where state and local government policies have set low tax rates and mandated a minimum of economic regulation. I say this should be no secret, except that little if any attention is ever focused by the national news media or by most Washington politicians on those state and local economies that are prospering and the obvious reasons why. The cameras and reporters always seem to be sent into the ghettos to bemoan the fate of their poverty-stricken residents, emerging with overwhelmingly sad stories and tragic statistics — but providing the nation with few answers as to how once-thriving localities deteriorated into poverty.

Burned into my mind, in this regard, is a piece CBS reporter Harry Reasoner did in 1982 on a run-down neighborhood in Camden, New Jersey, for the popular television program "60 Minutes." Reasoner's story covered all the predictable bases. He showed the slums, he talked to a local Catholic priest who anguished over the lives of his parishioners, he recited the grim statistics of appalling unemployment and urban decay and wasted lives. Yet not a question was raised, nor any satisfactory explanation given, as to how this community descended into an economic abyss. What drove the businesses and merchants away? What tax policies, zoning ordinances, and federal, state, and local economic regulations made this area an unattractive place to earn a dollar? What incentives were missing from this locality that could have drawn job-creating entrepreneurs and triggered increased opportunities? Harry Reasoner and his researchers apparently never asked, and thus "60 Minutes" never told us.

But if some of the national newspeople were to journey to other places in America where the economies are relatively robust, and where unemployment is very low, and if they were to ask the right questions, they would be able to reach some valuable conclusions about how poorer economies can be nurtured back to health. Consider, for example, the tiny state of Delaware. It is no mere coincidence that about half of America's Fortune 500 companies are legally incorporated there and that the number of jobs created by the banking and credit businesses went up sharply in Delaware in the midst of the 1981–82 recession. Delaware sought out these businesses and the jobs they brought with them by enacting economic incentives that encouraged financial companies and other corporations to move into the state. In 1981 the state government, under the leadership of then-governor Pierre du Pont IV, enacted among other things the Financial Center Development Act, which abolished usury limits for banks, wholesalers, and retailers, and implemented an attractive tax structure to lure big financial institutions. For instance, the first $20 million of annual income from operations in the state is taxable under Delaware's long-standing 8.7 percent tax on bank income. But for incomes over that, the tax falls in three stages to 2.7 percent on income above $30 million. "The taxes given up are ones that homegrown banks weren't able to pay," *Fortune* magazine observed. "In other words, to encourage economic growth the state lowered a tax rate that wasn't bringing in any money."

To further boost its overall economic climate and improve the state's debt-ridden fiscal position, Delaware has cut income taxes sharply since 1979, enacting three major tax cuts totaling 40 percent, along with two sweeping constitutional amendments. One amendment forbids the state government to spend more than 95 percent of projected revenues. The other amendment calls for a three-fifths vote in both houses of the state legislature before taxes can be raised or a new tax enacted. "As a result," says former governor du Pont, "old jobs have been retained and new ones gained. Delaware's growth of employment and income shifted from being one of the slowest in the late 1970s to one of the most rapid in the mid-1980s." Businesses are thriving in Delaware, with unemployment dropping to 4.3 percent by the end of 1985, the eighth lowest jobless rate in the nation.

Massachusetts is another example of how high state taxes force up prices, drive out businesses, and destroy jobs and economic growth. In the late 1960s and 1970s, the Bay State had deservedly earned the nickname Taxachusetts, and state officials saw companies relocating and jobs being created across the state line in New Hampshire, which has no income tax and no sales tax and, not surprisingly, one of the highest economic growth rates in the nation. Unemployment in New Hampshire stood at 2.8 percent as of the end of 1985. Then in 1980 a citizens' initiative — part of a nationwide antitax movement — succeeded in cutting Massachusetts's property taxes in half, triggering cries from critics that this would destroy the state's economy and gut needed government services. It was this tax cut that halted the job exodus, kept the state's renowned high-technology companies in Massachusetts, and created a new climate for economic growth. By the end of 1985, Massachusetts was enjoying the third lowest unemployment rate in the country, 3.9 percent.

America's ten lowest unemployment rates were in these states by the end of 1985:

1. New Hampshire, 2.8 percent
2. Maine, 3.8 percent
3. Massachusetts and Rhode Island, 3.9 percent

4. South Dakota, 4.0 percent
5. Vermont, 4.1 percent
6. North Carolina, 4.2 percent
7. Maryland, 4.3 percent
8. Kansas and Delaware, 4.4 percent
9. North Dakota, 4.5 percent
10. Connecticut and Nebraska, 4.6 percent

There were a number of factors contributing to the low jobless rates of these and other states, but the overriding factor among most of them is comparatively low business and personal tax rates. or, in the case of New Hampshire, South Dakota, and Connecticut, no personal income taxes whatsoever. Warren Brookes, the highly respected nationally syndicated economics columnist for the *Detroit News,* points out that in terms of economic growth, "Overall, the nation's 10 fastest-growing states raised their corporate taxes 95 percent but their personal income taxes only 22 percent" between 1970 and 1982. On the other hand, he notes, "the nation's 10 slowest-growing states did the opposite, raising individual income taxes a huge 77 percent, while holding corporate taxes relatively steady, with only a 10 percent rise."

Economist Richard Vedder of Ohio University concludes from this that "corporate taxes appear to have little significance to economic growth, while individual income taxes appear to be a substantial influence." However, he quickly adds this caveat: "Among the fast-growing states *both* corporate and individual income taxes are much lower than in the slow-growing states. For example, the 10 fastest-growing states had an average corporate tax rate (population-weighted) of $2.43 per $1,000 of personal income in 1982, compared to $6.85 [per $1,000 of personal income] for the slowest-growing states, so even though their corporate taxes had risen a huge 95 percent, they were still 60 percent below their slowest counterparts.

"At the same time," Vedder points out, "the 1982 individual income tax burden in the fastest-growth states was only $4.62 per $1,000, while in the slowest states it was nearly six times that level, at $24.67. So not only did the fast-growing states raise their individual income taxes very little, but they were already 85 percent below their slow-growth counterparts to start with."

It is equally significant that of the ten states with the fastest-growing economies between 1970 and 1982 — Alaska, Florida, Texas, Oklahoma, Nevada, Colorado, Arizona, Virginia, California, and Louisiana — four do not levy personal income taxes: Alaska, Nevada, Texas, and Florida. Among the ten worst-growth states — Ohio, Missouri, Wisconsin, New York, Massachusetts, Iowa, Pennsylvania, Maryland, Nebraska, and New Jersey — tax rates run as high as 14 percent (New York), and only two states, Iowa and Missouri, allow federal income taxes to be deducted. Moreover, all but one of the twenty-one states with the highest rates of new business formation and economic growth had below-average individual tax burdens, while a majority of the worst states for new business formation had above-average or rising tax burdens.

The positive effects of low individual state tax rates and an emphasis on small business growth are clearly illustrated by the jobs creation records of individual states. Compare the unemployment figures above to those of other states where taxes have been raised in recent years and where organized labor has in the past pressed excessive wage demands and restrictive hiring contracts. The best example of this is West Virginia, a heavily unionized, coal-mining state, in which there has been very poor economic growth and excessive state government costs and taxation. There the jobless rate was 12.6 percent by the end of 1985, the highest in the nation. Or consider the state of Ohio, where governor Richard Celeste doubled taxes in 1982, arguing that tax hikes were needed to help improve the state's economy and provide essential services. Instead the result has been a 9 percent unemployment rate, 2 percent higher than the national average, and a persistent record of poor economic growth.

Perhaps no domestic issue in modern American history has been more important, or more debated, than the issue of creating jobs. That issue continues to dominate today's national political agenda. And it boils down to this question: how can the economy's furnace be turned up to create jobs for every American citizen who wants to work? Since at least the New Deal days of Franklin Delano Roosevelt, there has never been a shortage of politicians who advocated government spending programs to create jobs. But the history of such programs has been a deeply disappointing one. Roosevelt established a myriad of public jobs programs during the Great Depression to "put people back to work," including the Civil Works Administration, the Works Progress Administration, the Public Works Administration, the Civilian Works Administration, the Civilian Conservation Corps, and the National Youth Administration. Many Americans who were given employment in these programs speak sympathetically of them today, often suggesting that similar government programs should be enacted now to provide jobs for the hard-core unemployed.

What is rarely mentioned, however, is the fact that although millions were employed by these government-funded programs, at a cost of billions of dollars, the unemployment rolls remained extremely high throughout the 1930s. "There is a popular misconception that Roosevelt . . . 'put people back to work,'" says George Mason University economist Thomas J. DiLorenzo in a study he conducted for the Cato Institute, a Washington-based public policy organization:

> The evidence, however, indicates that Roosevelt merely substituted government jobs for private sector jobs, as is always necessarily the case with government jobs programs. This made him very popular with the people who were given government jobs, but failed to alter the total level of unemployment throughout the 1930s.
>
> There were more people enrolled in federal jobs programs in 1938 than in any other year of the depression, yet the unemployment rate was still 17.2 percent in 1939 — *higher* than it was in 1931, a year before Roosevelt was elected to office and two years after the stock market crash.

Nevertheless, since that time there have been repeated attempts to lower unemployment and reduce poverty by mounting massive "public jobs" programs in localities across the country where the jobless rate was highest. And, indeed, hundreds of thousands of jobs were provided — but at an enormous cost to the economy and to the business sector. To pay for the costly government jobs programs that were begun under President Lyndon Johnson's administration required taking billions of dollars out of the cash registers and paychecks and bank accounts of the nation, money that would have produced real full-time jobs. As with the jobs programs of FDR's period, says DiLorenzo, "it is widely recognized that these modern programs have not created jobs but have simply enlarged the public sector at the expense of the private sector. In fact, there is evidence that the net effect of many jobs programs has been to *reduce* the number of jobs in the economy."

When Dr. Allen H. Gutheim of the Wharton Econometric Forecasting Associates testified before a House committee in 1982 on a major public jobs proposal, he had this to say: "The $5.5 billion House [jobs] plan would lift employment by 40,000 jobs by the end of 1984, far below the 320,000 the plan's sponsors forecast. And in 1983, the program would actually cost the economy 20,000 jobs as money customers would have spent elsewhere winds up paying for increased jobs." Nobel Prize–winning economist Milton Friedman went even further in a study of the legislation, arguing that the measure would actually result in the economy losing up to 100,000 jobs. Public jobs programs, "whenever they come into effect, would destroy more jobs than they create," said Friedman.

There are many other things wrong with public employment programs, including the fact that they often tend to be seriously abused by local political authorities, who see that their friends and political allies get the available jobs — as was frequently the case with the CETA (Comprehensive Employment Training Act) jobs of the 1970s. And government jobs training programs usually end up costing taxpayers more to provide each job than to send someone to a good four-year college or university. Writing about a 1982 jobs bill in the *New York Times,* reporter Ivor Peterson observed that "although the money was intended primarily to help men and women whose jobs had been in declining industries, the early beneficiaries of the fund have been the lawyers, accountants, engineers, and consultants brought in to draw up proposals, plan new projects and conduct public hearings on them." When the Office of

Management and Budget (OMB) examined the Local Public Works Program of the 1970s, the agency concluded that "only 12 percent of the jobs generated by the Local Public Works Program — and only 2 percent of the funding — actually went to persons previously unemployed." Furthermore, an OMB study concluded that public works jobs were costing taxpayers anywhere from $69,320 to $198,059 a year per job. The agency also found that from half to three-fourths of the jobs produced by public works projects went to generally skilled, most often unionized workers, benefiting few if any of the chronically unemployed or the poor.

The U.S. Department of Commerce's Economic Development Administration is perhaps the best illustration of a failed jobs program. Since EDA's creation in 1965, billions of tax dollars have been taken out of the economy in order to be redistributed to states and localities across the country in the form of grants for various public works projects and businesses. Yet there has been little if any evidence that such grants have effectively combated unemployment anywhere. In 1974 a congressionally mandated study of EDA concluded that the program was "inadequate in pursuing" its job-creating objectives, adding that it had made "only minimal progress toward the original objective of creating employment in areas of persistent, high unemployment." Congress chose to ignore that study and went on distributing billions of dollars in EDA grants to its constituencies throughout the 1970s and early 1980s. In 1985 David Stockman, the director of the Office of Management and Budget, took a fresh look at EDA, concluding that it was "a waste of money that doesn't create any net new jobs," and once again urged that it be abolished. "EDA project grants," says OMB, "lock resources into unproductive areas and industries, thus subsidizing inefficiency."

In 1848 Frédéric Bastiat, the great French economist, said this of government jobs programs:

> Nothing is more natural than that a nation, after making sure that a great enterprise will profit the community, should have such an enterprise carried out with funds collected from the citizenry. But I lose patience completely, I confess, when I hear alleged in support of such resolution this economic fallacy: "Besides, it is a way of

> creating jobs for the workers." The state opens a road, builds a palace, repairs a street, digs a canal; with these projects it gives jobs to certain workers. *This is what is seen.* But it deprives certain other laborers of employment. *This is what is not seen* . . . it is nothing but a ruinous hoax, an impossibility, a contradiction, which makes a great show of the little work that it has stimulated, *which is what is seen,* and conceals the much larger amount of work that it has precluded, which is *what is not seen.**

In times of economic depression and severe recession, it has been politically easier for many politicians and government officials to propose creating government-funded jobs. Easier, that is, in this respect: proposing the quick fix to combat unemployment is simpler than having to argue for the need for more sweeping tax and regulatory changes that would expand economic growth and eventually produce more jobs, real jobs. But the public jobs argument has been increasingly difficult to mount in recent years as the evidence has become more abundant that costly government jobs programs only serve to weaken the economy by further draining its capital resources; that even when government "creates" such jobs, the wheels of the legislative and bureaucratic process grind so slowly that the jobs come too little and too late in the ups and downs of the business cycle; and that the best way to create real jobs is to pursue economic growth initiatives — through tax rate reduction to encourage venture capital, and greater economic deregulation to sweep away barriers to business expansion and development.

On the other hand, acknowledging that more jobs can be created in a freer economic climate is still a far cry from the deregulatory and tax reduction steps needed to bring that about. In the previous chapter we saw how government-created obstacles effectively limit the economy's full job-creating potential. The task for those who believe that America's greatest years of economic growth still lie ahead is to identify and eliminate those obstacles and to implement policies that will permit vigorous and unrestrained economic expansion. Such a broad economic growth policy must be based on two major imperatives:

* Frédéric Bastiat, *Selected Essays on Political Economy,* ed. George B. de Huszar (Irvington-on-Hudson, N.Y.: Foundation for Economic Education, 1964), p. 16.

— Government spending must be restrained and tax rates must be reduced further to achieve the fullest possible levels of economic growth commensurate with the government's need for tax resources to maintain programs to guarantee national security and protect the general welfare of all Americans. A 1984 study on job creation and industrial growth by the Heritage Foundation, a highly respected public policy think tank, recommends: "Whenever possible, taxes and expenditures should be reduced to eliminate the deadweight loss that comes with the disincentive effects of higher tax rates."

— To encourage higher levels of economic growth, the economy must be further deregulated to allow the free market to produce and allocate resources in the most efficient ways possible. "Control of markets by federal pricing, taxing and purchasing policies has been a source of the country's" economic anemia, the Heritage Foundation study correctly concludes, "mainly because federal market intrusions have diverted private initiatives away from essentially productive activity associated with saving, working and investing and toward essentially counterproductive activity associated with lobbying the government for protection from competition and subsidies."

As America approaches the last decade of the twentieth century the economic miracle that is the envy of the world can be turned into an economic phenomenon. But before that can happen, indefensible regulatory and tax obstacles to increased job creation must first be swept away by government.

I'm not saying we won't have large companies but that we won't need them in many instances.

— *Professor Peter Drucker*
CLAREMONT GRADUATE SCHOOL

. . . the entrepreneur no longer exists as an individual person in the mature industrial enterprise.

— *John Kenneth Galbraith*
THE NEW INDUSTRIAL STATE

CHAPTER 7

The Myths of Big Business

MORE THAN A DECADE AGO Harvard professor John Kenneth Galbraith, a nationally recognized authority on economics and an advocate of socialism, predicted that the days of small business were numbered, a result of voracious giant corporations and multinational conglomerates bent on eliminating the competition. In *Economics and the Public Purpose* Galbraith suggested that small businesses were an anachronism. In other books he wrote that the entrepreneur no longer existed in large corporations; that creativity and innovation and new product creation were being smothered by the managerial class; and that giant corporations had become virtually immortal, immune from the slings and arrows of competition and business cycles. Perhaps no other single set of predictions and observations in modern economics has been so pitifully and misguidedly wrong as the ones Galbraith has set forth in a body of work noted as much for its myopia over corporate bigness and the "evils" of capitalism as for its obtuse, almost impenetrable prose.

On the contrary, the birth rate of new business enterprises has long been the single most arresting characteristic of the American economy. Not only has the fertile propagation of the small business sector been the most dominant fact in our modern economic life, but big corporate entities in numerous fields have seemed, for a time anyway, to be somewhat in decline. No one is saying, of course, that big businesses, however one defines that term, will disappear. Certainly, in the endless cycles of business growth and expansion, mergers and retrenchments, recessions and recoveries, big companies will always be a part of our economy — and an important part — offering economies of scale and volume from which all consumers benefit. But in recent decades the big U.S. corporations so feared by Galbraith have become a lesser force in the economic scheme of things. This has as much to do with the growth of the small-to-mid-sized business sector in a broad diversity of fields, especially the service industries, as it does with the rise of a global economy in which certain manufacturing sectors in the United States are being outperformed by competing nations, for example, steel and electronics from Japan or shoes and apparel from Europe and Asia. For these and other reasons, so-called big business no longer represents the heart and soul of America's economic infrastructure.

"There is no longer a premium on big size in many industries," economist and business management expert Peter Drucker told *U.S. News & World Report*.

> Companies pay a price for size; they are not very agile. Elephants can't turn on a dime, and neither can huge organizations with all their layers of management. I'm not saying we won't have large companies but that we no longer need them in many instances. For 30 years the trend was toward the large unit because it was the one we knew how to manage — or thought we did. That is over. We are deinstitutionalizing. You see it in the hospitals, where clinics now perform outpatient surgery. You see it in education, where the huge consolidated high school is being judged a failure. And you see it in business, where the spotlight is shifting toward the smaller unit.

> Politicians know this. The owner of a business employing 180 people can call his congressman directly and have more clout than can the Business Roundtable, which speaks politically for some of our biggest companies. But the Business Roundtable has to take unanimous positions, which means that it moves with the speed of the slowest and the wits of the dumbest.

Between 1970 and 1985, the American economy created 29.2 million new jobs — seven times more than our four biggest trading partners, Great Britain, Germany, France, and Japan. But while a record-shattering number of jobs was being created, the big Fortune 500 businesses during this period were losing 4 million to 5 million jobs. Most of them were being created by small, new businesses that, Drucker says, "absorbed all the post–World War II babies, and they absorbed the millions of women who entered the job market." Between November 1982 and November 1983 alone, according to economist David Birch of the Massachusetts Institute of Technology, the big corporations on the Fortune 500 list were losing 310,000 jobs while the overall economy was creating 3 million new jobs. The vast majority (70–80 percent) of these jobs, says Birch, "came from firms with less than twenty employees."

Nevertheless, in Galbraith's view, and the view of other antibusiness economists and activists, such as consumer crusader Ralph Nader, big business is virtually running America, manipulating consumers through mass advertising and largely determining the outcome of the U.S. economy. Giant corporate entities, moreover, "show marked indications of immortality," Galbraith declared in *The Affluent Society*. That, of course, would be news to big businesses that have either failed or come close to insolvency since he penned those words in 1958, for example, the Penn Central Railroad, Chrysler Corporation, and Lockheed, and many other large companies, such as Continental and Braniff airlines, and the Itel, Seatrain, Lionel, and Johns-Manville corporations, to name only a few.

But where Galbraith in his later works, such as *The New Industrial State*, completely misses the boat is in his belief that small businesses would no longer be a highly relevant and determining factor on the playing fields of the U.S. economy. Yet, as we have seen, it is among the major corporations and the smokestack industries that labor rolls have declined in recent years, while employment among small to mid-sized companies has rocketed into the stratosphere.

Nowhere can one find better examples of this incredible growth among smaller, entrepreneurial corporate entities than among the 500 small, privately held companies selected each year by *Inc.* magazine as the fastest-growing businesses of their class. They have names like All American Hero, a fast-food franchisor in Fort Lauderdale, Florida, which in 1985 *Inc.* rated the 15th fastest-growing company in the United States; Snappy Car Rental of Beachwood, Ohio, number 24; Jiffy Lube International of Baltimore, Maryland, an oil change franchisor, number 77; Ugly Duckling Rent-A-Car System of Tucson, Arizona, which specializes in renting old cars, number 176; and Megas Manufacturing of Cleveland, Ohio, which manufactures health and beauty aid products, number 351. They range from service-related companies like Phoenix Advertising, Design & Promotion, Inc., of Elm Grove, Wisconsin, ranked 500th, to American Trans Air, an airline based in Indianapolis, ranked number 7. There are companies like Weathervane Window Company, number 201, which manufactures wooden windows, and Fayette Manufacturing Corporation, which makes windmills, and was ranked 5th. From pizza parlor chains and waterbed companies to hearing aid manufacturers and home security system providers, the growth of these small, relatively new companies of the 1980s has transformed the American economy into one of greater diversity and abundance.

When *Inc.* magazine issued its annual list of America's fastest-growing small companies in 1985, the editors were astonished to see how much enterprises like these have grown in just the past five years. Their productivity alone, measured in terms of sales per employee, had shot up from $78,825 in 1980 to $185,850 in 1984. Average annual sales over these same five years had risen from $1 million to $14.8 million. The average number of workers per company jumped from 25 to 127. Another startling statistic: most of these companies were making money, with 456 of them showing a profit, 14 of them breaking even, and a mere 30 running at a loss. Notably, more than 200 of them were posting profits of over 6 percent. "These findings provide dramatic evidence once again of the extent to which growing companies have become the engine of the nation's progress," says *Inc.* editor George Gendron. "At a time when employment rolls of the corporate giants are shrinking, these 500 companies generated nearly 51,000 jobs in just the past five years. That's an average of over 100 employees per company on the list. When 100 new jobs are created in any community, that community benefits."

Thus, while some may look at the American economy and see only megacorporations and a slightly declining employment in the industrial and manufacturing sectors, others see that the lifeblood of the economy is being replenished by millions of small to mid-sized enterprises in cities and towns across America. Interestingly, more than 20 percent of the *Inc.* 500 companies, 101 to be exact, were located in California, where about 10 percent of the U.S. population resides. Texas was second, with 35 of the top 500 firms, and Virginia, with 30 companies, was third. New York, Ohio, and Florida each had 27 firms on the list; Pennsylvania came in seventh with 20. Massachusetts was eighth with 19. Ranked ninth was New Jersey, which had 18. In tenth place were Maryland, North Carolina, and Illinois, which each had 16 companies. In thirteenth place were Indiana and Washington State, with 13 firms each. Georgia, with 11 companies, was ranked fourteenth. Michigan and Tennessee each had 10 companies on the list.

Significantly, 74 of the up-and-coming companies resided in the so-called industrial Rustbelt region, including Wisconsin, Indiana, Illinois, Michigan, and Ohio — a testament to the fact that declining industries will be gradually replaced by new businesses and industries. Thirty-three companies on the *Inc.* 500 list were in New England. One hundred and five of those on the list, or 21 percent, were manufacturers or distributors of computer hardware or software, replacing lost jobs in other, older manufacturing industries, and over 40 percent of the firms were service-connected.

Thus, the static, monopolistic, megacorporate world of Galbraith and his economic disciples bears no relationship to the real business world of today, in which so-called big business is becoming increasingly irrelevant to the ebb and flow of the economy. The tides of job creation, venture capital formation, new product invention and innovation, and new marketing techniques are being pulled by the small companies of today that will become the big companies of tomorrow. While economists and politicians during the 1960s and early 1970s were myopically concentrating on the rise and fall of major corporations as the principal factor in job creation and the relative health of the Gross National Product, small businesses were becoming the real workhorses of the economy. A study by MIT economist David Birch discovered, for instance, that while small, independently owned U.S. companies with fewer than twenty employees represented about 33 percent of total employment, they were responsible for creating two-thirds of all new jobs in this country between 1969 and 1976. In terms of job creation alone, big business was no longer king.

One need only look at a number of thriving state economies to understand how big business has taken a backseat to small businesses in the current period of economic recovery and growth. Nowhere, perhaps, can one find a better example of the driving growth forces of small businesses than in the state of New Hampshire. As noted earlier, economically it is one of the fastest-growing states in the country, yet the state's average number of employees per firm is only six. Even so, between 1970 and 1984, job growth in New Hampshire was double that of the rest of the nation. Moreover, New Hampshire's personal income growth was 76 percent greater than the national average.

Similarly, with an average of eleven employees per firm and a job growth rate almost double the national average, North Dakota is another example of small business potential. Yet despite the lack of major industries, its income grew 33 percent faster than the national average during the 1970–84 period.

On the other hand, states with a predominant number of big businesses did much worse. High-tax New York, for example, with forty-four employees per firm, had a job growth rate 93 percent below the national average and real income growth 47 percent below the national average. Or consider the state of Illinois, which is heavily industrialized. With an average of forty employees per company, Illinois had a job growth rate that was 87 percent below the national average and an income growth rate that was 47 percent below average. Obviously, as pointed out in an earlier chapter, excessive state tax and regulatory policies are also a significant factor in the relative health and prosperity of each state's economy. Yet at the same time, the states that have enjoyed vigorous job and income growth are those in which there has been substantial growth among small business enterprises.

"Recently emerging trends in our economy have increased the importance of small firms," says Bruce D. Phillips, senior economist within the Small Business Administration's Economic Research Office. Not only has the growth of small to mid-sized businesses displaced big business as the pivotal job creator in America's economy, their growing numbers and their flexibility have given our economy new "shock absorbers," says Phillips, cushioning it against future recessions so that it will be able to bounce back with greater resiliency. Most entrepreneurs whose enterprises fail soon reincorporate new businesses and try again. "This greater flexibility has meant that they have been able to take advantage of new market opportunities faster than large firms, e.g., their movement into the newly deregulated markets in trucking, air transportation, financial services, and communications during the past several years," he says.

If one can point to any sector of the economy where small has come to dominate big, it is certainly in the retail markets. We have become, says a 1985 headline in *Inc.* magazine, "a nation of shopkeepers." And contrary to Galbraith's view of corporate immortality, the big urban retail chains have been very mortal indeed in the face of growing competition from the small independent shops and chains. Chains like Korvettes have gone out of business, while other giant retailers like Montgomery Ward have closed down many of their stores across the country, victims of specialty stores that are selling everything from homemade ice cream to children's clothing. In any major business district in cities both large and small, the proliferation of specialty shops and malls has been the single most visible change to occur in the nation's retail market — from downtown areas in Washington, D.C., and St. Paul, Minnesota, to refurbished waterfront areas in Baltimore and Boston. More than fifteen years ago, for example, St. Paul's Grand Avenue was a depressing two-mile stretch of business real estate, pockmarked with little but auto repair garages and car dealerships, a victim of the consumer's flight to the city's surrounding suburban malls. Today, the colorfully merchandised windows of nearly five hundred specialty stores line the avenue, to which thousands flock to stroll and shop and eat.

The numbers tell much of the story of the retail industry's David and Goliath struggle, in which small businesses are seizing the lion's share of the retail market: between 1977 and 1982, the major department and variety stores grew by only 37 percent. Over this same period, specialty store sales rose 56 percent. Categories in which specialty stores are breaking the bank and the backs of many big retail chains: infant and children's clothing sales went up 92 percent; toy and game shop sales jumped an incredible 112 percent; bookstore sales rose 82 percent. In short, the big business chains are no longer dominating the retail market. Small retail businesses comprising four stores or less now hold a 55 percent share of the overall retail industry. Among specialty stores, the dominance is even greater. Independently owned stores, for example, have captured 70 percent of the sporting goods and bicycle market; 60 percent of the food and drink business; and 78 percent of the market in infant and children's clothes.

"General merchandisers are getting their heads kicked in by specialty stores," says a New York City business executive. Among the shopkeepers that have successfully challenged the big department and variety store giants are the Gap Stores, Inc., which specializes in clothing for youths; Crabtree & Evelyn, a chain of perfume and toiletry shops; and Steve's Ice Cream, Inc., which began with a single shop in Somerville, Massachusetts, in 1981, offering unique new flavors, and plans to have some three hundred stores around the country by 1988. Take that, Howard Johnson's!

In *The New Industrial State*, published in 1967, Galbraith found little in the corporate hierarchy worth celebrating. All entrepreneurial creativity, he suggested, was being smothered by a robotic managerial class, or what he called the Technostructure. "With the rise of the modern corporation," he wrote, "the emergence of the organization required by modern technology and planning and the divorce of the owner of the capital from control of the enterprise, the entrepreneur no longer exists as an individual person in the mature industrial enterprise." But in point of fact, big businesses increasingly have been encouraging employees to develop new products and even new enterprises within the corporate structure — to the point of providing them with start-up capital within the corporation to develop new subsidiaries of their own creation. One reason for this is to keep the company's best and most creative employees from leaving to start their own businesses. Steven Wozniak, for example, was once a 25-year-old computer designer at Hewlett-Packard, one of the giants in the computer industry. But Wozniak left to start his own company when Hewlett-Packard officials rejected his idea for developing a microcomputer that could be hooked up to a home television set, the forerunner of the personal computer. Wozniak went on to pursue his idea and together with Steven Jobs helped launch Apple Computer, which rang up sales of $1.5 billion in 1984.

For this reason, more and more corporations are trying to foster the spirit of entrepreneurship within their companies by giving their employees the time and the resources to pursue and develop their own ideas. Management consultant and author Gifford Pinchot III has coined a term for it: Intrapreneurship. "The more rapidly American business learns to use the entrepreneurial talent inside large organizations, the better," Pinchot says. "The alternative in a time of rapid change is stagnation and decline." But in addition to being given the time and resources, Pinchot says, employees must also be given independence from the corporation's bureaucracy. Even if big companies are good at coming up with bright ideas, they are generally poor at carrying them out because of a "morass of analysis, approvals, and politics" throughout the corporate hierarchy. Some prime examples in which major corporations have encouraged intrapreneurship:

— When General Motors established the Saturn Corporation, a separate company from the main GM structure, to produce its new subcompact, GM chairman Roger Smith said he wanted Saturn to be free of GM's entrenched, bureaucratic procedures. To wit, Saturn Corporation will have its own engineering, design, and marketing staffs, and it will also be able to negotiate a separate labor contract with the United Auto Workers.

— The 3M corporation now allows its employees to spend up to 15 percent of their time on independent development projects. That helped 3M chemical engineer Arthur Fry, who used 3M scientist Spencer Silvers's accidental discovery of an adhesive with very low sticking power to make what eventually became Post-it, the popular small tags with the adhesive edge that can be stuck to anything but leave no mark or residue when removed. At first Fry's idea went nowhere in the huge corporation, but he persisted and succeeded in breaking through the corporate bureaucracy. 3M began selling Post-its in 1980, and sales are now running about $100 million a year.

— When General Electric named Jacques Robinson to run its lackluster video products division, he immediately declared his door open to anyone with new ideas. One person who walked through his door was Howard Stephenson, Jr., who had burned the midnight oil in his home workshop to design circuitry that brought standard television sets up to monitor quality.

— Five years ago IBM Corporation, the Goliath of the computer industry, adopted the concept of independent business units (IBUs), which were set up to operate as separate organizations. IBM's most famous IBU was the one responsible for producing the corporation's popular personal computer. But in the process of developing the home computer, the company's IBU broke some of IBM's most sacrosanct customs. Significantly, it decided to bypass IBM's famous sales organization and sold the PC through retail stores. Equally significantly, it also bought most of the parts from outside suppliers. Today, IBM's PC has been one of the industry's extraordinary success stories, and the dozen people in the original IBU that developed the PC have grown to more than 10,000.

Throughout our industrial history, "Big Business" has been the convenient whipping boy, not always without justification, for a host of political, organized labor, consumer, and environmental groups. And the attacks continued unabated throughout the 1960s and 1970s. They reached a fever pitch in the mid-1970s when the late Senator Henry "Scoop" Jackson, Democrat of Washington, a highly respected figure in the U.S. Senate, called U.S. oil company profits "obscene" and proposed that the government take over oil exploration and drilling on public offshore drilling sites. Many politicians were ready, and still are, for that matter, to raise taxes on business in general in the belief that such taxation would have no impact on anyone other than wealthy corporate entities. What such politicians, and the economists who support them, invariably fail to point out is that businesses do not really pay taxes, they merely collect them from consumers in the prices they charge for their goods and services. Raise taxes on business and you increase prices and make America's goods and services less competitive both here and abroad, hurting consumers at home who are least able to afford higher prices, as well as workers whose jobs would be lost as a result of reduced sales. Moreover, by raising taxes on business, you drain away scarce investment capital needed to finance plant modernization, expansion of the work force, and, eventually, better pay and benefits for America's workers.

But times are changing. Indeed, the changes in political and social attitudes toward the business community in general have reached a point where the president of the United States could publicly question, as Reagan did in the early 1980s before a group in Boston, the usefulness and wisdom of levying corporate taxes at all. "I'm not sure we should even have a corporate tax," Reagan said in a moment of unguarded candor. That doesn't mean that the corporate tax is in danger of being abolished anytime soon, but great reforms often begin when someone has the courage to suggest that a law or custom is no longer relevant to the times.

What has changed, most certainly, is the role of big business in the American economy. No longer is it the engine that drives the economy's job-producing machine. No longer is it the wellspring of technological advances and marketing innovations. No longer is it the center of the nation's economic infrastructure. A Dun & Bradstreet Corporation survey found that in 1985 U.S. businesses expected to hire an additional 2 million workers, 53 percent of which would come from firms employing fewer than one hundred people. In sharp contrast, during this same period the Fortune 500 corporations were producing almost no new jobs. The big-business Goliath that John Kenneth Galbraith and his disciples have devoted their academic careers to scarifying and regulating, is dead — cut down by a diverse, ever-expanding, increasingly competitive capitalist economy.

I was 66 years old. I still had to make a living. I looked at my Social Security check of $105 and decided to franchise my chicken recipe. Folks had always liked my chicken.

— *Colonel Harland Sanders*
FOUNDER, KENTUCKY FRIED CHICKEN

In any real and living economy, every actor is always an entrepreneur and a speculator.

— *Ludwig Von Mises*
HUMAN ACTION

CHAPTER 8

The Entrepreneurial Spirit

WHILE TRAVELING THROUGH AMERICA IN 1831, Alexis de Tocqueville observed that "America is a land of wonders in which everything is in constant motion and every change seems an improvement." Across the vastness of the American continent, "no natural boundary seems to be set to the efforts of man, and in his eyes what is not yet done is only what he has not yet attempted to do," the great French writer said.

It is this constant striving to improve, to attain the previously unattainable, to build enterprises both great and small that so impressed Tocqueville, and these qualities are what have made America a land of everlasting opportunity. At the very core of America, now and throughout its history, lie a boundless spirit of optimism about the future and an almost religious belief in the value of hard work and the benefits that can be derived from such effort, both for the individual and for the common good. America has achieved its greatest periods of economic growth, as it did, for example, in the late 1800s and early 1900s, when the free market incentives for personal achievement and the accumulation of wealth were greatest. But as with all human endeavors among nations, leadership is also an integral part of spurring a nation to greatness and helping to unleash and motivate its economic power. Even the most irrepressible spirit of optimism and drive can suffer dispiriting setbacks and periods of depression; but it will rebound in response to the proper stimuli.

In this sense, nations, too, can respond with greatness in the face of adversity if their leaders understand the need not only to lead but to encourage and motivate. Winston Churchill surely understood this in the early 1940s, when Great Britain and its people were being relentlessly pounded by Hitler's war planes and rockets. He declared that the British people would "never give in. Never. Never. Never." President Franklin Delano Roosevelt, presiding over one of the bleakest periods in modern American history, realized upon winning the presidency during the Great Depression that America's will and potential were still strong and that more than half the battle of restoring the economy was psychological. He sought to buck up the American spirit when, in perhaps the most memorable statement of his presidency, he told a temporarily dispirited and depressed nation that "the only thing we have to fear is fear itself."

In much the same way, Ronald Reagan also realized the need to rally the spirit of the American people as the U.S. economy sank into the Great Recession of 1981–82. Besides his economic growth prescriptions of lower tax rates, less economic regulation, and restraint in spending, Reagan also understood the need for the president to be both a teacher and a national cheerleader to rally and encourage the American spirit. After the tumultuous and largely leaderless decade of the 1970s, when the nation had been racked by the Watergate scandals and the deep divisions over the Vietnam War, and had been told by Jimmy Carter that it had lost its spirit, Reagan sensed the need for renewal and rededication of the nation's spiritual and economic strengths. "Besides being its leader and commander in chief," Nevada Senator Paul Laxalt, Reagan's close friend and confidant, says, "he also understood the need to be a teacher, instructing the nation about the inherent strengths of its economic system, and, like FDR, reminding Americans that they had nothing to fear; that the recession would go away; that America would come back; and that this country could do whatever it set its mind to doing."

Through his personal appearances, televised speeches, and weekly radio chats with the nation, Reagan was as much a national therapist as he was the chief executive. Yet from the very beginning of his presidency, this side of Ronald Reagan seemed to totally mystify much of the national news media, which could not understand his use of dynamic models to describe the economy. Instead of talking in cold, clinical, macro terms about the economy, responding to this or that stimulus, Reagan spoke in terms of individual human action, of each American's limitless potential, and of the value of hard work, a free economy, ambition, and striving for a better life for one's family. Reagan talked repeatedly of the need to "renew optimism and confidence and rekindle the nation's entrepreneurial instincts and creativity." Yet the Keynesians at the *New York Times*, for example, didn't know what to make of this approach to the economy. To them, it all sounded like "psychonomics," an editorial said. Indeed, said the *Times*, it seemed that Reagan was administering "group therapy" to the business community and the nation at large.

This of course was exactly what Reagan was doing, believing like Theodore Roosevelt and FDR and JFK, among other activist presidents, that the presidency must be a rallying point for the nation in times of adversity and struggle. More than three years after assuming the presidency, when the economy had rebounded from the recession, Reagan talked about the psychology of the economy in a radio address to the nation on March 10, 1984, in which he partially answered his mystified critics at the *New York Times:* "I remember saying back when things looked worst that too much pessimism could be deadly. Well, some people criticized me for trying to sugar-coat bad news. I merely wanted us to remember that there's a psychological factor in recession, and too much hammering at it makes recession worse. What pulled us through that ordeal, I'm convinced, was our determination to stick to our program, belief in ourselves, and trust in our values of faith, freedom, and hard work — values that have never failed us when we've lived up to them."

An incurable optimist who devoutly believes in the untiringly industrious America that Tocqueville so much admired and chronicled, Reagan steeped his presidential addresses in an almost religious worship of the values of free enterprise and the heroism of entrepreneurial risk taking. Many people have spoken and written about America's entrepreneurial spirit and the dynamics of its free market. But no one in the 1980s more eloquently captured its infectious spirit and even magic than did Reagan in innumerable speeches, especially one he gave to the students and faculty of St. John's University on March 28, 1985. In that speech he said this:

"When you make out your taxes, you claim one exemption for yourself. And you find that once you've worked for a year, that between federal taxes, state taxes, city taxes, social security and sales taxes, you're giving over thirty percent of your entire $20,000 salary to taxes — more than $6,000.

"Now, I could argue the morality of this, of your paying so much and involuntarily finding yourself in a condition of something approaching servitude. And I will. But I wish, right now, to speak of broader practical purposes.

"If you were allowed to keep more of your money, you'd likely do one of three things with it. You could spend it on a portable computer, say, or clothing, or entertainment, and thereby stimulate the economy to hire more computer, clothing, and entertainment makers, thus creating jobs. Or you could save it and add to the pool of capital from which banks lend money, thereby stimulating the economy by making capital available for businesses to grow. Or you could be very creative and invest your money in a private enterprise.

"Now, some of you are only a generation or two removed from the immigrant experience. Some of you are the grandsons and granddaughters of sharecroppers who came north for jobs. Many of you are the first in your family to go to college. I was the first in mine, and I, too, am a grandson of immigrants. All of you came from hardy, risk-taking stock, and you're very much the sort of people who would in a few years take the few thousand you'd gain from a tax cut and pool it with friends and acquaintances in order to invest it.

"Twenty of you might put up as much as $5,000 each and start a business — a local newspaper, a small record company, a service industry, a small computer firm — whatever. And that expands the economy, creating new businesses, new jobs, and new wealth. This is the magic that is and always has been at the heart of America's economic strength.

"We have lived through the age of big industry and the age of the giant corporation. But I believe that this is the Age of the Entrepreneur — the Age of the Individual.

"That's where American prosperity is coming from now, and that's where it's going to come from in the future. . . .

"The technological revolution has seen to some of the things that I'm talking about. We have to recognize that and encourage the brave men and women who are taking risks in investing in the future — they ought to be honored. But to invest your time and money and concern is a leap of faith — a profoundly hopeful act that says, yes, I have faith in the future; I am the future; the future is what I make it."

There is in Reagan's vision of the American entrepreneur a wonderful universality as well as a purposeful recognition of the almost mythic heroism in each would-be entrepreneur's need to dream great dreams and overcome all obstacles to achieving them. Perhaps more than any other modern president, Reagan has both understood and expressed the deepest economic and even altruistic entrepreneurial motives in the American psyche — the need to build something beyond oneself, to provide something that fulfills a need in society, or simply to change the way things are, to change the future. More than that, Reagan has also understood that entrepreneurial expansion can be encouraged through national leadership, that he could through moral persuasion inspire the nation to take chances, chase its dreams, and realize its fullest human potential. "We are all, then, entrepreneurs and speculators in one degree or another," says Dr. William H. Peterson, director of the Center for

Economic Education at the University of Tennessee. "Nobody is immune to the opportunities and uncertainties that life unfolds before us. Entrepreneurship is a normal human capacity. It can be cultivated and developed. It is a possible dream."

It is this inescapable and unarguable possibility of entrepreneurship, that the dream can be realized, that gives it its universal allure, its immortality. Though thousands have tried and failed before, thousands more have succeeded, and thousands more will try again and fail and yet still try again, stubbornly believing that this time their enterprise will succeed, that it will win the approval of the marketplace. This, perhaps more than any other aspect, is what makes entrepreneurialism so endlessly fascinating and, as Reagan dares to suggest, so heroic. This is the spirit that pushed Steven Jobs in his garage at night to perfect the personal computer, believing that while no one out there was asking for a home computer, they would once they came to understand what it could do. This is the idea that gripped Ray Kroc, founder of McDonald's, as he looked out and saw a nation of hamburger stands but believed that his idea for a fast-food franchise would revolutionize the industry. This, too, is the dream that captured Joel Hyatt's imagination as he envisioned a nationwide chain of low-cost legal offices for the masses — in a nation already awash in lawyers — that would, he promised, take "the fear out of legal services."

Within this perhaps indefinable spirit of entrepreneurialism beats not only the heart of our economy but the future Ronald Reagan talked about — America's future. For somewhere out there, working in a garage or a basement workshop, is tomorrow's Steven Jobs, tinkering with a bit of bizarre technology that may end up producing an endless source of high intensity energy; or a biomedical researcher in a laboratory who will devise an implantable lens to make the blind see, or produce a cure for cancer. Or it may be something far less revolutionary than that, perhaps just another addition to our growing service industry that no one thought anyone could possibly need or want, but which will eventually produce 400,000 new jobs. The list of possibilities is endless and relentless — almost as relentless as the tide of American entrepreneurs, which never seems to stop rising. In 1950 there was an average of

1,800 new business start-ups per day, says author Gifford Pinchot III. By 1960 the number of new business formations was averaging about 4,000 per day. By 1983, the number had multiplied three-fold, to an estimated 12,000 per day. Today that entrepreneurial spirit is alive and well and growing.

I lit my lamp beside the golden door!
— *Emma Lazarus*
"The New Colossus"

CHAPTER 9

Entering the Golden Door

Rosa Alexander is a black entrepreneur who pulled herself out of poverty through her indomitable determination to succeed and her tireless capacity for hard work. She has achieved wealth and the admiration and respect of her community and her peers, and she did it the old fashioned way. She earned it . . . by scrubbing floors.

Alexander and her four sisters grew up in the poor, rural cotton- and tobacco-growing farm country of Dunn, North Carolina. Her father was a lumberjack and her mother worked as a domestic; the couple separated when she was young. Though she completed high school, her dreams of going to college were foreclosed to her by economic circumstances that she describes simply as "hard times." Nevertheless, she says, her mother instilled in her children the belief that they could achieve anything they wanted in life if they worked hard enough for it. Rosa Alexander never forgot her mother's advice. And for the next twenty years this self-described "go-getter" worked very hard as a restaurant manager in a Ford plant, an aircraft cleaner at a naval air station, and as a part-time janitor.

"I was fifty," she says, "and I was working for this man who knew little about the cleaning business. I was running everything for him. Finally, I said to myself, 'This is stupid. I'm doing all this for him and I can't do it for myself?' " Remembering what her mother taught her, Alexander quit her job in 1978 and risked $16,000 in personal savings to start her own cleaning business, beginning with a few mops and pails and two employees. Today, her Norfolk, Virginia, cleaning company, A&B Janitorial Service, provides work for nearly three hundred people — some of whom she's pulled off welfare — and grosses nearly $3 million a year. Continuing to work seventeen-hour days, Rosa Alexander still occasionally scrubs floors just "to instill in my employees that I am no better than they are and that there is nothing wrong with hard work and helping others."

In 1979 Theodore N. Holmes opened up a small fast-food restaurant in Baltimore, giving it the unlikely name of Chicken George, after the resourceful and ambitious black slave in Alex Haley's best-selling novel *Roots* who earned enough money to buy his family's freedom. Holmes, a black entrepreneur from York, Pennsylvania, had spent two years researching and taste testing to develop his restaurant's unique fried chicken, putting in sixteen-hour days to make his fledgling enterprise a success. By 1982 Chicken George had mushroomed into a successful chain of eight highly profitable restaurants in Baltimore, Philadelphia, and Washington, D.C., earning $14 million a year in sales and becoming one of the top one hundred black-owned companies in America.

Mr. and Mrs. Duk Shim left their homeland in Seoul, Korea, in the early 1970s for a new life in the United States to increase their children's chances for a good education and a better way of life. After they settled in Washington, D.C., Mrs. Shim worked as a nurse's aide and her husband, who gave up a job as a construction manager before emigrating to America, found work as a wallpaper hanger and started a newsstand. It wasn't long before the Korean couple had saved enough money to open a small Capitol Hill restaurant, which they run with the help of their son, 25-year-old Byung, a cousin, and one employee. By 1985 the Shims were not only prospering, they were moving ahead with plans to open another Washington food business. Their son, who was majoring in accounting at nearby George Mason University, was nurturing plans to someday start his own business. Byung's sister, Hyun, a student at Virginia Polytechnic Institute, was seeking a degree in computer science. "Here in America," says Byung Shim, "you can open a business very easily. There are lots of opportunities."

Frank Sepulveda was a poor young Mexican-American with big dreams for the future who worked for a San Antonio wholesale produce company in the mid-1950s. But this hardworking son of an immigrant was restive and unhappy in his job, wanting to implement ambitious plans to expand the company, plans that his employer wouldn't approve. One day, while he was venting his frustrations to a California potato supplier whom he had befriended, the businessman asked Sepulveda why he didn't start his own business. When he replied that he didn't have the money to undertake such a venture, the businessman shot back, "I'll lend you $50,000. If you make it, pay me back. If you don't, don't worry about it." When a surprised Sepulveda asked why he would take a chance on him, the businessman explained that his father, a banker, had told him that if he ever had a chance to help out a Mexican, do it. "They're sincere," his father told him, "they're honest, they'll work hard, and they'll never let you down." In a few days a $50,000 check arrived in the mail, but soon afterward Sepulveda was stunned to learn that the businessman had died. His attempt to return the money was rebuffed by the man's mother. "He wanted you to have it," she told him. "You do what he wanted you to do with it."

Sepulveda used the $50,000 to start his own produce business, putting in long, backbreaking hours to make it succeed. Today, more than thirty years later, this immigrant's son is the owner of one of the biggest wholesale produce companies in the country. He has long since paid back the $50,000 venture money he received from his unselfish benefactor and in turn has become one of San Antonio's major philanthropists.

Youa Her fled her native country, war-torn Laos, in the mid-1970s, seeking a land where she could live in peace and realize her fullest potential. With the help of a refugee assistance group, Her settled in Wausau, Wisconsin, where she opened Zuag's Gift and Grocery Shop. In addition to selling Asian groceries and other foods, Her sells lovely traditional Laotian art stitchery to her customers.

As soon as she came to the United States, she knew that she

wanted to run a business of her own. "I figured that in this country, everybody is running businesses," she told a reporter for *Inc.* magazine. "We can go without money for a little bit, but not without food. That is what made me come to start a grocery business." How did this would-be entrepreneur without any capital find the means to start her enterprise? At first, she sought advice from the Chamber of Commerce but found their material "too confusing." Deciding, finally, to strike out on her own, she traveled to St. Paul, Minnesota, and talked to some established Laotian food retailers about lending her food to sell at 10 percent below retail cost, arguing that they could expand their sales through her business in Wausau. They agreed and lent Her about $11,000 worth of merchandise, which she sold in only three months. From that point on, her well-stocked grocery store and gift shop was on its way toward becoming a viable business.

The remarkable and inspiring stories of Rosa Alexander's cleaning business, Theodore Holmes's fast-food chain, the Shim family's restaurant, Frank Sepulveda's produce business, and Youa Her's Asian grocery collectively represent the story of America. Their experiences tell of people who have risen out of poverty through their own gritty determination to succeed, fostered by an unshakable belief that they can achieve anything they set their minds to doing.

More people have come to our shores or crossed our borders to live and work here than have entered any other country in recorded history. They and their children have prospered as no peoples have ever prospered anywhere else in the world. Germans, Italians, English, Irish, Hungarians, Canadians, Russians, Mexicans, Cubans, Swedes, Poles, Koreans, Chinese, Japanese, Vietnamese, and many others have come to America by the millions from every corner of the globe, seeking opportunities and a better way of life for themselves and their families. From the early settlers in the 1600s and 1700s to the great waves of migration from Europe and Asia in the nineteenth and early twentieth centuries, they have woven the richly colored and resilient fabric of America's economic life. Through their skills and ambitions and their inexhaustible labor, they built businesses, factories, and industries and in the process helped to create and nurture families and neighborhoods, towns and cities, schools and churches, and the greatest charitable and philanthropic institutions the world has ever known. They made the economic promise of America a living, breathing reality.

The stories that began this chapter, like the timeless stories of America's early immigrants, are the stories of people who made America great, stories of poor or low-income minorities who have found opportunity and reward within America's free economy, and who have in turn made the free market work for the benefit of all. Though they tell of incredible singlemindedness of purpose, of courage in the face of adversity, and of driving ambition, their stories are in fact commonplace throughout our country. They are to be found in every state, city, town, and hamlet, and among every minority group. Yet strangely, relatively little attention is paid by the national media to the thousands of poor or disadvantaged Americans — native-born as well as foreign-born — who are continuously lifting themselves out of poverty and climbing the rungs of the economic ladder. On the other hand, a great deal has always been made — and deservedly so — of the plight of the poor, whose numbers rise and fall with the nation's economic performance. The little-acknowledged reality of America's low-income populations is the continuing process by which so many so-called disadvantaged people, through their own talents and initiative and ambition, enter that "golden door" which Emma Lazarus's words immortalize on the base of the Statue of Liberty.

All too often, unfortunately — perhaps as a result of the relentless stream of Dickensian stories visited upon us by the mass media — we have come to stereotype the poor and minorities as some sort of permanent subclass in our economy, incapable of increasing their income and rising out of their impoverished circumstances. The days when immigrants and native-born disadvantaged persons could make it on their own seem, to some at least, to be out of a romantic bygone era. Yet today, just as in earlier times, one continues to see innumerable examples of people who have worked their way out of poverty. Indeed, the statistics available in recent years provide much evidence that the "golden door" is not only still open to all who wish to enter, it is growing wider to accommodate the increasing numbers of people who are crowding through. Consider:

— In 1982, according to the U.S. Census Bureau, black Americans owned 339,239 businesses. Although this number is pathetically small in comparison to the 14 million businesses and 26 million blacks there are in America, it nevertheless represents a significant 47 percent jump from the number of businesses blacks owned in 1977. Moreover, gross receipts for black-owned businesses were up by 44 percent, from $8.6 billion in 1977 to $12.4 billion in 1982. Service and retail trade industries account for about two-thirds of all black-owned businesses.

— Between 1970 and 1980, the number of women, blacks, and other minorities who held professional and managerial jobs nearly doubled, according to a study by the Potomac Institute, an independent, nonprofit research organization that says it is "concerned with equality of opportunity in American life."

Among those holding employment positions classified as "officials and managers," blacks increased from 1.9 percent to 4 percent, and Hispanics increased from 1 percent to 2.2 percent. Over this same period, the proportion of "professional" jobs held by blacks increased from 2.5 percent to 4.3 percent; Hispanics' share of such jobs rose from 1.1 percent to 1.9 percent; and the number of such positions held by women rose from 24.6 percent to 37.2 percent. Blacks and other minorities also increased their share of construction trade apprentice positions from 10.6 percent to 19.3 percent.

— From 1972 to 1982, according to more recent federal statistics, the number of blacks holding jobs classified as managers and officials shot up by 83 percent to 445,000.

— Between 1980 and 1982, sales revenues for the 51 biggest Hispanic companies in the United States rose by 47 percent, while the Gross National Product during this same two-year period rose by 16.7 percent. In 1982 sales for the nation's top 100 Hispanic businesses averaged $35.7 million, and the average for the top 440 Hispanic firms was $11.25 million — a whopping 280 percent jump over their 1977 sales, which averaged $2.96 million.

— Overall, an eighteen-month study of Hispanic businesses by the U.S. Chamber of Commerce's National Chamber Foundation found that Hispanic entrepreneurs were making extraordinary strides in the nation's marketplace. "Quietly, steadily, Hispanic-Americans have been on the move, building businesses, making jobs, creating wealth," the study concluded. "They have proved themselves [people] with talent and drive, and a taste for success. They show every indication of being a stimulus to the economy in the coming decades and a vital resource for growth." Said an official who worked on that study, "The best-kept secret in the United States is what has happened to the Hispanic business community in the last decade."

— More than 700,000 Indochinese refugees — Vietnamese, Cambodian, and Laotian — have flocked to America in the last decade, prospering faster than any previous groups of immigrants within recent memory. "They've shown a remarkable ability to enter into mainstream American economic life," says Brandeis University professor Lawrence H. Fuchs, an expert on immigration and refugee policies. "Rarely have so many come so far, so fast," concludes an investigation by the *Wall Street Journal*. "Indochinese refugees are graduating from West Point and founding high-tech firms in Silicon Valley. They are taking over shrimp fishing in Galveston Bay and mom and pop stores in inner cities. They are reviving seedy urban areas in Arlington, Virginia, and in San Francisco's Tenderloin."

— The president's 1985 report to Congress on the state of small business reached this conclusion:

> Minority interest in business ownership is increasing. Small, minority-owned firms are showing an ability to take advantage of business opportunities and to compete successfully in the marketplace with a degree of profitability and success that is attracting additional financing for their start-up efforts. Since 1977, minorities have responded positively to public and private incentives to participate more in business ownership. The percentage of nonwhite persons in self-employment has increased [and] nonwhites have gained in self-employment in relation to wage-and-salary jobs, although to a lesser degree than whites.

— In 1977, according to the president's report, "41 nonwhite persons were self-employed for every 1,000 nonwhite wage-and-salary workers. By 1983 there were 45 self-employed nonwhite workers for every 1,000 nonwhite wage-and-salary workers, an increase of 10 percent. The comparable increase for white persons was 14 percent during the same period."

In short, there have clearly been some significant strides made in the business community by minorities, especially blacks. Though the national and local figures for unemployed black youths, as I've previously pointed out, are a disgrace, overall black employment is up. During the two years of economic recovery following the 1981–82 recession, black employment climbed by 1.3 million and represented 18.1 percent of the net increase of 7.2 million in total civilian employment. By the end of 1985, blacks held 10.7 million jobs, constituting nearly 10 percent of total employment. Since the recovery began in 1983, blacks have gained about 40,000 new jobs a month, and between 1983 and 1984 alone, some 400,000 blacks have risen out of poverty.

At the same time, black entrepreneurs are entering the marketplace in growing numbers and succeeding. In fact, many blacks holding middle-level executive and managerial positions in the business world are leaving corporate America to start enterprises of their own. A 1984 investigation by the *Wall Street Journal* discovered that "black managers climbing the corporate ladder are finding that it often doesn't reach as high as they want to go. Many are jumping off to start their own businesses, betting that they can rise higher and faster as entrepreneurs." Says Roosevelt Tabb, a director of the National Black M.B.A. Association: "Partly it's the American tradition of wanting to do your own thing, and no different than the direction a lot of white middle managers are taking. But it's also a reaction to color barriers in big companies. Ambitious blacks don't want to wait until the year 2000 to be named executive vice-president."

The Census Bureau reports that between 1973 and 1983 the number of blacks that were self-employed in nonfarm occupations jumped by a surprising 51 percent to 506,000. In sharp comparison, the number of self-employed whites rose by "only" 29 percent over this same period. Among metropolitan areas, the Los Angeles–Long Beach area boasts the largest number of black-owned businesses, 23,520; followed by the New York City metropolitan area, 20,242; the Washington, D.C., area, 18,805; Chicago, 13,660; and Houston, 12,206. This rapid growth in black entrepreneurship has been one of the least-noticed entrepreneurial developments of the past decade. Consider these examples:

— Artie Johnson's Detroit rib business began to falter in the early 1980s. Many of his patrons could no longer afford the $7 price of a rib dinner. Instead of closing down, however, Artie and his family decided to change their menu from ribs to hamburgers. Johnson, along with his son and daughter, obtained an $85,000 loan and bought and renovated an old gas station. Yogi Burgers soon opened, with twelve employees, in July 1982. Yogi's grossed $325,000 in 1983, providing enough cash to expand to a second restaurant in downtown Detroit. Sales tipped $400,000 in 1984 and were expected to double in 1985.

— Walter Delegall's Crescent Computer Systems is unique in that it is one of the few computer companies operating out of Harlem. "Many customers, black and white, are uneasy about coming to Harlem," says Delegall, but the expertise and training provided by Crescent overcomes that fear. Delegall started Crescent in 1980 with $5,000. His company did $310,000 in sales in 1984 and was projecting $500,000 in sales in 1985. Delegall credits his success to providing people with "good service."

— Angela DeJoseph began ADJ Enterprises, a Chicago-based public relations and image consulting firm, with an answering machine and $8,000 in savings. Despite a $30,000 contract with one of the nation's largest black advertising agencies, ADJ lost $20,000 in its first year. Determined to make it, DeJoseph worked harder and fought to keep her business going, eventually earning a very high reputation among her clients for her services, especially among black cosmetics companies. ADJ grossed more than $250,000 in 1984 and has coordinated print and television advertising aimed at black consumers for M&M products, Coca-Cola, and Johnson cosmetic products. "The main ingredient for success is hard work," says DeJoseph.

— Danny Dukes was one of Detroit's few black millwrights, installing conveyors and other machine equipment. He worked his way up from apprentice to superintendent in ten years before deciding to quit the company he worked for and start his own business. He founded Danny-Dukes Machinery-Conveyors in 1983 with $4,000. His initial investment has produced a company with ten employees that grossed $225,000 in 1984. Says Kathleen White, the company's vice-president, "All we need is work, we don't need any handouts."

— When Caroline Jones worked for the J. Walter Thompson advertising agency in 1968 she was making $75 a week and going nowhere in the secretarial pool. Determined to make something of herself, she took a copywriting course and became the New York agency's first black woman copywriter. In the beginning, she admits, "I didn't know what I was doing. But I showed up for work every day, which a lot of people who don't know what they're doing don't do, and I kept plugging and learning." A series of jobs with a number of major advertising agencies gave her the broad range of experience she sought and led to a vice-presidency at Batten, Barton, Durstine & Osborn. But she knew that this was as far as she was going to go on the corporate ladder. That's when she decided to strike out on her own to co-found the Mingo-Jones Advertising agency in 1977 with two black vice-presidents from two other agencies, bringing along two major ad accounts with them. "We were the three highest-ranking blacks in the business in New York, the cream of the crop," she says. Today, the Mingo-Jones agency has more than a dozen clients, including Miller Brewing Company and Kentucky Fried Chicken, and boasts gross annual revenues of some $22 million. "I did not have any role models, but I also didn't have anyone telling me that what I wanted to do was impossible," Jones says.

America is still very much the land of opportunity for immigrants as well. "The labor market experiences of the foreign born are part of the 'success story' of America," says a 1985 analysis by Ellen Sehgal, an economist for the U.S. Department of Labor's Bureau of Labor Statistics. "Studies of the foreign born show patterns of economic difficulties in the first years after arrival, but substantial upward mobility thereafter."

The tendency among many immigrants to take entry-level jobs in the economy and then gradually work their way up the economic ladder is as true today as it was in earlier periods of U.S. immigration history. According to Sehgal, a study by David North of a group of 1970 immigrants revealed

> that, for a few years after arrival in the United States, many were in jobs of a lower skill than those they had held in their native country. North found, for example, that there had been a sharp drop in managerial and professional employment among the immigrants. After several years, however, there was an increase in the net number of professionals (that is, those who formerly were in professional jobs and those new to such occupations). By 1977, the proportion of immigrants who were managers, proprietors, and owners exceeded the average for native-born workers.

Interestingly enough, Sehgal's analysis shows that in 1982 the foreign-born group with the highest median annual earnings, $12,200, were Asian-born immigrants. Workers of Asian ancestry who were born in the United States also registered the highest earnings among various nationalities, $13,281. Equally noteworthy, a healthy 30.3 percent of foreign-born Asians and 26.1

Table 2
FAMILY INCOME OF $35,000 AND OVER
(APRIL 1983)*

	Native-born (percent)	Foreign-born (percent)
White	20.5	16.8
Black	17.0	29.9
Hispanic	10.9	7.0
Asian	26.1	30.3

Source: Ellen Sehgal, "Foreign-Born Workers in Labor Market," *Monthly Labor Review*, July 1985.
*Figures apply to families with at least one member in the labor force.

percent of native-born Asians enjoyed annual incomes of $35,000 and above.

The story of T. Young Suhr, a young Korean who left his homeland in 1969 to become a teacher in America, illustrates the resourcefulness and entrepreneurial talents that so typify the Asian immigrant. As it happened, even with a master's degree in education, Suhr was unable to find employment as a teacher in Los Angeles. However, determined to make his own way here, he started selling automobile parts to Korean-owned service stations out of the trunk of an old car. Working day and night, he and his wife gradually expanded their auto parts business, purchasing an abandoned store in a run-down section of Los Angeles in 1974 for $7,000.

In the years that followed, many other Koreans came to America seeking a better life for their families, with many of them settling in the same run-down Los Angeles neighborhood where Suhr had opened his business. Nicknamed Koreatown, it has become something of a mecca for small Korean enterprises, many of them doing business with their native country. Recognizing there was a need for a hotel in the area that could serve visiting Korean businessmen, Suhr obtained loans from two banks, tore down his auto parts store, and built a $2.1 million hotel on the site. He opened his Western Inn in the summer of 1984, and it has been a huge success ever since.

Many Asian entrepreneurs have pursued the American dream by opening their own small retail businesses and working from dawn to midnight to make them succeed. In most cases they are family-run enterprises, with the husband, wife, and other relatives working side by side. Though such long hours often leave parents little time for their children or a regular home life, they are willing to work seven days a week if necessary in order to give their children a better home and the opportunity to go to good schools and pursue professional careers. Is it worth it? Yes, says *Wall Street Journal* reporter Earl C. Gottschalk, Jr., who observes that "the Koreans' success in the U.S. demonstrates that the nation's ladder of upward mobility still works. Even in low-tech, unglamorous, small retail and service businesses, the Koreans have proven that hard work, attention to detail and the entrepreneurial spirit can still pay off."

All of this is in no way meant to suggest that all poor persons or disadvantaged minorities are able to pull themselves out of poverty solely through hard work and a dream. Nor do I mean to say that there aren't appalling instances of poverty in many places in America that remain untouched by economic growth, or that there aren't poor or low-income people who come to this country who never make it. Clearly, many people through no fault of their own are poor — the abandoned elderly, the infirm, abandoned mothers with young families to support, people who are mentally ill and homeless, the chronically unemployed — and who need society's help. Indeed, as graphically pointed out in earlier chapters, their circumstances are frequently made worse because government obstacles to economic growth have foreclosed numerous economic opportunities that would help many more poor and low-income people to become self-sufficient.

What is clear, however, is that millions of poor and low-income people who were born here or emigrated here do make it, despite these and other obstacles. America today is a cornucopia of untold stories that give eloquent testimony to this immutable fact. Indeed, the preceding stories and statistics show that the promise of America, opportunity for all who seek it, is still very much alive and attainable. More important, these stories illustrate that when entrepreneurs strive to lift themselves out of poverty and succeed, they open up innumerable opportunities for others within the marketplace. The success of each business begets more economic opportunities and more jobs, and many of those who work for these successful enterprises are in turn encouraged to begin their own enterprises — just as Rosa Alexander and Frank Sepulveda and countless others have done. And on and on it goes in an unending stream of entrepreneurial growth, business formation, and job creation for the benefit of all.

At the same time, there are other all-too-frequently unnoticed dividends in all of this. Rosa Alexander's decision to go into business for herself did much more than just make her a relatively wealthy woman, allowing her to move into a big, comfortable home and provide a better life for her five children. It enabled her to hire poor and low-income people within her area for whom there were few or no job opportunities until Alexander created them through her ambition and skill as a businesswoman and as an employer. Her first clients were a doctor's office and a day care center, then she landed a $49,000 janitorial contract with the local naval air station. When the navy accepted her bid for a $1.9 million contract to clean the Norfolk Naval Shipyard in Portsmouth, Virginia, plus a contract to clean several military commissaries, she immediately went out and hired eighty-five women who were on welfare. Her success turned her enterprise, as it does with countless other enterprises, into an effective weapon against poverty — providing real jobs and opportunity for people who had little or no training or skills for meaningful employment.

Furthermore, Alexander's financial success has enabled her to channel surplus capital into other worthwhile public endeavors, including plans to develop low-income housing for blacks and other area residents. Meantime, she has contributed generously to Norfolk State University and has attended graduation ceremonies where she quietly handed out envelopes containing $1,000 checks to five NSU graduates who had worked for her part-time. It is her way of saying "I'm proud of you and your accomplishment, now go out and make something of yourself." Multiply such unselfish, altruistic acts by thousands of other businesspeople like Rosa Alexander, and the limitless potential of entrepreneurial growth to help poor and low-income people to help themselves becomes immediately clear.

The continuing saga of economic opportunity and individual achievement in America is exemplified in the lives of people like Rosa Alexander and Frank Sepulveda and innumerable others, immigrants and native Americans alike, in the dreams they dreamed and in their ability and determination to make them come true. The fulfillment of such aspirations is a wonderful, everyday reality for millions of Americans as well as millions more who come from foreign lands seeking to enter our golden door. But the doorway of opportunity is not as wide as it should be. This is why we must work to widen it even further for all who still seek the American dream.

If you do have an entrepreneurial voice that's calling out to you to try something new, to do something, listen to it. And then if you really are going to embark on your own business, be ready for long, hard work.

— *Linda Richardson*
PRESIDENT, THE RICHARDSON GROUP

You don't need all the business skills in the world. You need some intelligence. To some degree, you can learn the business skills, but if you have a very clear idea and you know what you want to do and you have your product, by God, go do it.

— *Lane Nemeth*
PRESIDENT, DISCOVERY TOYS

CHAPTER 10

Enterprising Women

THE EXPLOSION IN THE NUMBER of women in the work force during the last two decades has not only significantly altered, and elevated, the role of women in our society, it has also sparked a phenomenal growth in the number of woman-owned businesses — nearly 3.5 million companies by last count and climbing rapidly.

This growing corps of female entrepreneurs has strongly contributed to the remarkable rate of new business formation in America and promises to further revolutionize the makeup of our economy, propelling more women into major executive and management positions throughout the corporate infrastructure. Nurtured and encouraged by the economic growth of the 1980s, the number of women entering the business world is multiplying at a breathtaking pace. Consider these statistics:

— In the last ten years, more than 24 million new jobs have been created, two-thirds of them going to women; nearly 54 percent of the female population is working, up 10 percent in the last decade; according to the Bureau of Labor Statistics, female participation in the labor force will surpass 60 percent in the next ten years.

— Of the 7.3 million new jobs created during the 32-month period between December 1982 and August 1985, nearly 50 percent were filled by women.

— Women made up 36 percent of the work force in 1972. But by 1984 they constituted 44 percent of the work force. Between 1972 and 1980, their numbers saw a 10 percent increase among better-paying white-collar jobs, while dropping from 16 percent to 11 percent among blue-collars.

— While women are entering virtually every sector of the economy, increasingly they are entering, and in many cases leading, the U.S. economy's fastest-growing sector, the service industries, holding 60 percent of all service sector jobs.

— Women made up only 22 percent of the nation's managerial, administrative, and executive positions in 1975. By 1985 they held 34 percent of these positions. Moreover, when *Inc.* magazine compiled its annual list of the nation's five hundred fastest-growing privately held small to mid-sized companies in 1985, twenty-three of the chief executive officers (CEOs) on the list were women.

— Meanwhile, their numbers are also growing in largely male-dominated professions: women constituted 13.6 percent of the legal profession in 1980. By 1984 they made up 16.1 percent of it. They made up 13.3 percent of the number of physicians in 1980, but that jumped to 16 percent by 1984. The number of woman economists increased by 10.3 percent during this same period.

— Among nontraditional jobs, women have made even greater gains in the last thirteen years, according to the Bureau of Labor Statistics. The number of woman construction workers has nearly tripled. Woman truck drivers have doubled. Women in protective service professions have nearly tripled. The number of female mechanics and repairpersons has grown tenfold.

Yet it is the amazing growth in the number of new woman-owned businesses that has become a phenomenon in today's economy. Though many woman-owned enterprises germinated and took root in the 1970s, their businesses really began taking off in the entrepreneurial era of the 1980s. *Today, woman-owned small businesses represent the single biggest source of new business formation in the United States.*

But such statistics reveal nothing of the heroic struggles, the financial obstacles, and countless other hurdles that a growing army of enterprising women have had to surmount in order to succeed. They have started businesses as diverse as chocolate cookie factories, toy companies, and construction firms. They have come from all walks of life and every educational background. Virtually all of them are enormously self-confident, determined to succeed, filled with unbounded energy, and possessed by an idea that they believe will fill a need and at the same time make money.

"A little voice told me to do it on my own," explained Linda Richardson, a kind of corporate Joan of Arc, who followed that voice. After resigning from her job at Manufacturers Hanover Trust Company, one of the world's ten largest banks, she set herself up in business in Philadelphia doing the same thing she did for Manufacturers Hanover — training bank employees in sales and marketing techniques. Today, her company, The Richardson Group, grosses $2.5 million annually. Though she's happy with that, Richardson expects even greater growth in the future.

Setting up a business of her own was not an entirely new experience, she points out. "I've always had an entrepreneurial streak." While still in college, for example, she sold antique jewelry to stores like Bloomingdale's and Henri Bendel of New York. Later, equipped with a master's degree in psychology, she ran a private school and then became a principal of an alternative high school in the 1970s. But after deciding that ten years of working in schools was enough, she answered the call of Manufacturers Hanover. Her task: to set up a sales training program for bank employees. At the outset, though, she found that the old generic approach to selling was not appropriate for the world of banking. General selling tips, she discovered, "are very useful, but it's not enough just to know the process of selling." You have to know the products and customers, too. A customer has to feel comfortable with your explanation of a line of credit or a sophisticated financing method. She felt she could offer that kind of training better on her own.

So, after one year at Hanover, Richardson took the plunge and went into business for herself, establishing The Richardson Group, with Manufacturers Hanover as her first customer. The timing couldn't have been better. As a result of banking deregulation and new competitive pressures, financial institutions were offering a whole range of new services for the first time. The Richardson Group offered to fill the banking industry's need for experts to teach their employees how to sell their services. By 1982 Richardson's firm was generating around $1 million in annual revenues, 15 percent of which was profit. Today, with twenty-five employees and around $2.5 million in revenue annually, she says proudly that her firm is "considered one of the best in the world."

Part of Richardson's secret of success is something she says she learned when she taught English courses: all aspects of a sales program must be integrated. Too many training programs don't take into account the participant's experiences and needs. As a teacher and company president, she reminds banking professionals that "people don't come in as blank slates. You have to build on their prior experience and knowledge."

Constantly on the road as a speaker, she says her husband, a radiologist at St. Agnes Hospital in Philadelphia, is "very supportive" of her career. What motivates her? For one thing, her love of education and selling. For another, her unquenchable fascination with the broad range of banking services spawned by deregulation, which has blurred the distinction between investment banks and other financial institutions. But perhaps the single most important ingredient in her enterprise's success is her willingness to work hard. She frequently worked until ten or eleven o'clock at night in the early days of her business. "It takes tremendous effort and tremendous dedication,'' she says now. ''It's really hard work, but it's not labor.''

What is her advice for other women thinking about starting a business of their own? ''The first thing is to recognize your own entrepreneurial drive because no one really tells you that you're an entrepreneur. You have to recognize that you may be a little different, and trust yourself. If you do have an entrepreneurial voice that's calling out to you to try something new, to do something, listen to it. And then if you really are going to embark on your own business, be ready for long, hard work. You have to be organized. And I really think the key, at least in my business, in the service business, is to understand all aspects of delivering your service, especially for start-up. If you want to start up a business, and if you are good at all the pieces, at the very beginning you're going to be called on to do many of the other pieces. For instance, in my training company, I started out training, designing training, delivering training, and training trainers.''

To succeed in business ''you really have to have an idea and a market,'' she continues, ''and a way to differentiate what you're doing. I found a niche not through offering very broad-based training, and this was deliberate. I selected one area of training that I was very interested in because I love training.'' Moreover, ''you have to support yourself during the lean time,'' she says. ''You have to be prepared to understand what the investment is going to be, what it will take to maintain the business, what it will take to support yourself through the almost always slow start.'' And for a while it didn't look as if her company was going anywhere. After she landed Manufacturers Hanover as a client, it took her six months to close the next deal. Her secret: ''Resilience and enthusiasm. You have to be the kind of person who can spring back if there's a disappointment, not to take it personally but to learn from something that doesn't work out and continue to move forward.''

Linda Richardson is a perfect example of the kind of woman entrepreneurs who are becoming a major factor in an explosion of new small to mid-sized companies. According to President Reagan's 1985 report to Congress *The State of Small Business,* ''women-owned businesses are the fastest growing segment of the small business population." In 1977 fifty-two out of every one thousand people were nonfarm proprietors. Forty-two percent of these fifty-two business owners were women. By 1982, however, there were sixty-three nonfarm sole proprietors for every one thousand people. Fifty-one percent of them were women.

Women's share of total business receipts grew modestly in this same period, though they still fell short of the average of all nonfarm sole proprietorships. Accounting for 7.8 percent of receipts in 1977, women's share grew to 9.6 percent in 1982. In dollar figures, 1977 receipts for woman-owned nonfarm businesses totaled $25.2 billion. In 1982 they totaled $41.7 billion.

Net income for all businesses owned by women grew from $4.2 billion in 1977 to $5.2 billion in 1982. By 1984 woman-owned businesses accounted for 9.4 percent of all nonfarm enterprises, or around 3 million companies — up from 1.9 million in 1977.

As women enter the business-ownership world in increasing numbers, they are in a sense repeating the tried-and-true methods of America's immigrants of the early 1900s who rose to the top of their professions, says Charlotte Taylor, a Washington-based consultant and author of *Women and the Business Game*. Women are "the new immigrants," she says. Just as their ancestors of both sexes faced unfamiliar customs in the New World, women are facing new practices in the fields they are entering for the first time. And just as the entrepreneurs of old started their own businesses to avoid hiring or promotional prejudices, so women have started theirs to avoid being typecast by employers whose judgments of women may be based on prejudicial information. Until women are corporate leaders in far greater numbers than they are today, many executives will base their opinions of merit on the work they have come to expect from women with little business experience. Thus, the only way up is often the way out, as women jump off the corporate ladder to create corporations of their own.

Though women obviously are still not yet strong in traditionally male-dominated occupations, that's rapidly changing as they continue making gains in such male bastions of the marketplace as construction, law, dentistry, pharmacology, finance, broadcasting, and the print media. In the construction industry, for example, there were 10,000 self-employed women in 1972. By 1982 there were 37,000. One of them is Mary Farrar.

When she began her own construction company in 1978, she was following the advice of a man she describes as "the oldest hippie I'd ever met. Old Charlie," she recalls, used to philosophize quite a lot while she worked for him as a part-time tax accountant in the 1960s. He couldn't help noticing how hard she worked, putting in the same diligence in handling the company's tax returns that the firm's owner might have, had he been called upon to do the work. "I had a tendency to put my whole self into it," she says. So when Farrar decided to become a bookkeeper for a Kansas City construction company, a job that soon had her doing everything the absentee owner didn't do, old Charlie advised her, "If you're going to work that hard, you might as well own a piece of it."

But when she asked the company's owner if she could buy into the firm, he turned her down. Within a month, however, using $500 in savings, she had formed a company of her own, starting out by erecting steel frames for warehouses with the help of a contractor friend. Though the job brought in only $250,000, an amount she's since surpassed many times, "it seemed huge to me then," she says. During the eight years she was employed at the other construction company, she had helped erect small buildings ranging from 6,000 to 8,000 square feet on the average. This contract called for a building covering 100,000 square feet. As "the new kid on the block" and "the wrong sex to boot," she was thrilled at the opportunity.

Farrar began by recruiting laid-off workers, obtaining thirty days' credit from suppliers, and working out an agreement with her contractor friend to be paid in weekly installments instead of the usual thirty days. There was no turning back. Her company, Systems Erecters, Inc., was officially launched. Though the weather during the entire project was "god-awful," she managed to get the warehouse built just as the customer wanted. And she prospered until the 1981–82 recession hit, dealing a major blow to her company and the construction industry generally. "It was a nightmarish experience," she says.

That's when she decided to start a second company, one that offered a broader range of contracting services, a one-stop construction center that would handle zoning, find building sites, hire architects, and do the general contracting as well. Soon her new firm, Hallmark Construction, began building apartments for doctors and other upper-income professionals looking for tax shelters. By 1983 the company's revenues hit $2 million. Today, her companies together are generating around $4 million in gross revenues.

Not every business decision worked out well, however. In 1984, as an experiment, Farrar took on a new worker — her husband. A sheet metal journeyman, he thought he'd enjoy heading up the new company's field division. Unfortunately, it wasn't long before they jointly decided that their twenty-eight years' worth of experience at making their marriage work had no relevance to their working relationship. Unlike a case in which a husband and wife start a company together, "it was an unusual situation for a husband to come into," she says. "By their nature, they're husbands. They've got to tell the little wife how to do things." By January 1, 1985, they had decided to go back to the old arrangement of being just husband and wife. "And things are much better now, thank you," she says.

As with any highly competitive business, particularly the construction business, "there's a tremendous amount of stress," Farrar says. "Still, if you're a very high-energy person, it gives you the opportunity to do as much as you want to do." Besides, working for someone else usually means less involvement than you want or a smaller reward for your efforts, she explains. With five adult children, she hopes one of them will soon join her in the management end of her construction business. One of her sons already works in the field. "Ten years ago, people were very surprised to meet a woman who owned a construction company," she says. "Today, however, women are losing their touch at surprising people."

Mary Farrar's fierce drive and a stubborn determination to succeed against all odds are among the chief hallmarks of the entrepreneur. Sandra Hunt, too, has that kind of drive, instilled in her by her father, who constantly told her when she was growing up, "You can't just grow up and get married. You have to make something of yourself." At the age of 15 she began saving up for college and helped put herself through the University of Texas by working two jobs. Earning a bachelor of science degree in biology, she set out to make her mark in the world but soon found it wasn't going to be easy. "Whenever I got tired," she reflected, "I kept telling myself that J. C. Penney made and lost three fortunes before he made one he kept. I hadn't even made one yet."

In 1972, at the age of 27, she bought the equipment of a failing medical lab where she worked and went into business for herself, providing microbiological testing for food outfits. And along the way she innovated. Her company helped motivate employees toward greater cleanliness by suggesting bonus plans to employers. When clients said they had difficulty getting food samples to her firm, she started operating a courier service. She grossed $54,000 in her first year and $1 million in 1982.

Unfortunately, not every decision worked out as she had hoped. While she was seeking an M.B.A. degree, business instructors advised her to diversify; she made a disastrous stab in some electric car and silver mine investments and saw $50,000 go down the drain. But failure being one of the greatest teachers, she learned from that day on to follow her instincts. "I'll never again get into something I can't control," she says now.

In 1983 Hunt merged her Bio Search lab with another firm, Professional Service Industries, Inc., a Chicago-based company with $40 million in sales and more than eight hundred employees. Sandra Hunt is now a vice-president and a major Professional Service Industries stockholder, with six of the company's fifty labs under her authority. One of her main jobs is finding new sites for the company's testing operations around the country. "Giving me more markets," she says with characteristic enthusiasm, "is like giving an alcoholic the key to a liquor store."

Giving the key to a cookie store to a self-confessed "chocoholic" might be equally dangerous if you weren't dealing with the now-famous Mrs. Fields. If "Famous Amos" is America's king of the ultrarich, ultraluxurious chocolate chip cookie, then Debbi Fields, founder of Mrs. Fields Cookies, is its queen. It was her love of chocolate that sent Fields in search of the "ultrachocolatey" chocolate chip cookie recipe. When she found it, she says, she decided to take a shot at opening a cookie store in her hometown of Palo Alto, California.

Despite advice from friends who said there was no future in cookies, her husband, an economist and investment counselor, plunked down $50,000 worth of faith in her idea. But though he supported her financially, she didn't want to rely on him for advice. To prevent that, she read every business book she could get her hands on. She needed the expertise, she says, because at the time "people were hesitant to buy cookies they could bake for themselves at home."

To change such ingrained buying habits, Fields hit the promotional cookie trail, handing out cookies on the street for a free sample, and giving passersby a taste of what they were missing at home. It worked, and by 1985 Mrs. Fields had seventy stores on the West Coast, Hawaii, and in the Midwest. Ten stores were scheduled to open in New York City, while other outlets were planned for Florida, Australia, and the Far East. Today, her cookie empire brings in revenues of $30 million a year. What's Mrs. Fields's secret of success? "I use nothing but the best ingredients," she says. "My cookies are always freshly baked. I price the cookies so that you cannot make them at home for less. And I still give cookies away."

The growing movement of women into the U.S. labor force is a well-known phenomenon, accelerating substantially in the 1960s and even more rapidly in the past decade. What is a relatively newer phenomenon, at least in terms of its surprising growth, is the number of women who now occupy management positions in business. True, as of 1985, no woman held the position of chief executive officer of a Fortune 500 company, with the exception of Katharine Graham of the Washington Post Company. Mrs. Graham took over her husband's position when he died. Still, a greater proportion of women today are in management-related positions than ever before. In 1984, in fact, 45 percent of all company managers were women, up from 39 percent in 1983.

In education, the figures also look promising. "The number of women who received bachelor degrees in male-oriented fields skyrocketed from 1976 to 1982," writes Carole Bodger in *Working Woman* magazine's Sixth Annual Salary Survey of 1985. There was a 531 percent increase in engineering degrees and a 200 percent increase in degrees in business. From 1972 to 1982, the proportion of degrees held by women in law grew from 7 to 33 percent and in medicine from 9 to 25 percent. Women also earned 28 percent of the M.B.A.'s awarded in 1982 — 29 percent more than they received in 1971.

President Reagan's 1985 report *The State of Small Business* adds that women in 1982 earned 4,470 out of 17,900 science and engineering Ph.D.'s, representing an annual gain that was one of the largest since 1973. About 83 percent of women's doctorates were in psychology, life sciences, and social sciences. Only 3 percent were in engineering. But with a 90 percent gain in the number of full-time female undergraduate engineering students between 1978 and 1983, the report forecasts a large future expansion in the number of engineering doctorate degree holders who are women.

Three fundamental characteristics permeate the entrepreneurial revolution among women — ambition, persistence, and an extraordinary talent for spotting a moneymaking opportunity. Sharon Poindexter, the first black president of the 1,600-member National Association of Women Business Owners, has all of these qualities and much more. Her consulting firm, Poindexter Associates, grossed around $400,000 a year. Her clientele included the Association of Bank Women, the National Board of the YWCA, and Ultissimo Skin and Body Salon.

She started her business in Wichita, Kansas, in 1971, but moved to Kansas City, Missouri, in 1982 to take advantage of the greater business activity there. Then in 1984, she began the research for a new company, Chrysalys Corporation, to produce video programming on management topics for hotels and community colleges. Now that the production phase is complete, she's working on marketing and sales and hopes to have her first buyers soon. Confident of success, she points out: "There is no one yet producing a management program. There are of course some things on television that are news magazine format or they deal with business subjects, but no one concentrates specifically on management."

Poindexter learned her first business lesson from her grandmother, "Mamaw," back in Hutchinson, Kansas. "Mamaw had a sharp eye for opportunity," she says. Besides cleaning homes for five families during the week, she did hair on Fridays and Saturdays and "every month would send someone down to Louisiana to bring back a load of buffalofish to sell to all the Louisiana folk who lived in Hutchinson. If she was real short of cash, she would sell pies."

As the president of the National Association of Women Business Owners (1983–84), Poindexter saw her role as one of helping women climb the ranks from Gal Friday to corporate manager and to business owners. She has especially sought to help black woman entrepreneurs. "Black women come from a business heritage," she believes. "To me, all those greasy spoons, hairdressing salons, and barbecue stands reflect our ability to be incredibly enduring. We persevere consistently. I've found incredible spiritual strength in acknowledging that power."

Many woman entrepreneurs have joined forces with their husbands to establish new enterprises, often right in their own homes. Consider the story of Avis Renshaw, 26, and her husband, Steven Cox, 37, of Herndon, Virginia, who in 1981 faced a $750,000 bankruptcy. A farm loan had fallen through, droughts had ruined their crops, creditors had begun screaming for payment. "It didn't cross our minds to go on welfare," says Cox. That "would have been a horrible rut to fall into." His wife agrees. Though several of her friends were accepting unemployment compensation, she thinks that alternative is "low. You work at McDonald's if you have to," she says. So instead of crying for the government to bail them out, they embarked on a business that is as American as, well, as apple pie, because that's what they've been making and selling successfully ever since. It was a decision that saved them from financial ruin.

They began by selling their unnamed pies in local farmers' markets in order to make ends meet, and experimenting to find the best combination of recipes that would make their pies distinctive and irresistible. Gradually, sales began to climb. Renshaw was expecting her second child when a local farmer insisted she had to give the pies a name. "Mom's," she said simply, and it stuck.

Today, if you walk into a Safeway supermarket in the Washington, D.C., area, one of the 5,000 pies made by the couple and eighteen co-workers will quickly attract your attention. The reason: they just don't look like store-bought goods. In fact, you might wonder if a local homemaker just wandered in and left a few on the shelf by mistake. For one thing, Avis Renshaw and her husband use only fresh ingredients in their pies. When the recipe calls for lemon juice, for example, they use real lemons. For another, the crusts don't have that stamped-out look, but have a thick, bubbly, uneven appearance, the kind that you probably remember your mother or grandmother making. "The imperfections are their strength," Cox says. And no fancy multicolored packaging disguises them, either. The pies are wrapped in cellophane and come in a wide variety, including apple, blueberry, peach, chocolate chess, and nearly a dozen others. By 1984 Mom's Herndon, Virginia, pie company was grossing $800,000 a year.

As is generally the case for new entrepreneurs, their first years were hectic, but for more reasons than running their business. They also had to take care of three small children, Clancy, age 5, Ansa, 3, and Petey, 1. Yet driven by what they call "the embarrassment factor," Renshaw and Cox managed to put in sixteen-hour days month after month to pay back what they owed family and friends. They still remember the first time they made twenty-five pies in one day, sleeping in four-hour shifts so the pies could keep baking in what was then limited oven space.

As their apple pies began to "sell like hotcakes," Renshaw says, they began adding other pies, then breads and fruitcakes to their line of baked goods. The fruitcake attracted the notice of Washington business consultant Adrienne Arscht, who insisted, "I can do better," when Bloomingdale's executive vice-president Lester Gribetz asked her to taste what he planned as the department store's Christmas fruitcake special. Ten pounds' worth of taste-testing later, Arscht discovered Mom's. As the first shipments were sent off to New York, the delighted consultant helped set up Mom's Pies as a corporation, retaining a 20 percent interest. Plans are in the works for Mom's Pies to be frozen and distributed to supermarkets far outside the Washington, D.C., area. But purists needn't worry that the pies' natural homemade flavor will change. Cox, who supervises the production while his wife handles delivery and the paperwork, says he won't add preservatives or additives to the pies, and freezing them, he explains, leaves the quality untouched.

Like all entrepreneurs, the couple has a confident and upbeat vision of what their business will be in the future. One day they would like to see it become a "Knott's Berry Farm East," with 50,000 pies produced each week, sweet corn picked the very day it's put in bins, and baked goods made from wheat the company grows itself. "I think all these things are possible, and I'd like to prove it," says the soft-spoken, black-bearded farmer-turned-piemaker.

In common with many other working mothers across America, Barbara Adamek was desperate to find a nanny to care for her child while she was busy at work. Her 6-year-old "refused to go to after-school day care" after three years in the same program, she recalls. But rather than give up, Adamek turned her frustration into a unique idea — a nanny business that grossed $250,000 in its third year — and now teaches others around the country how to do it, too.

Back in 1981, before she began the company, Adamek was working for an Atlanta advertising firm and looking for the kind of nanny who was as "highly educated" and caring as the one who cared for her when she was a little girl living in Rochester, New York. Contrary to her mental picture of the Old South, there weren't legions of nannies looking for jobs. Though only 23 percent of mothers with children under 18 worked at the time, compared with over 70 percent today, Adamek says she couldn't immediately find the right person for her child's "creative talents and needs." About that time, "the guilty-mom syndrome took over," she says. But she soon realized that she couldn't be "the only frustrated professional woman in the city of Atlanta who had this feeling." If she needed a good nanny, so did many other working mothers. And thus Nanny Pop-Ins was born. In her first year of business (1981) providing insured and bonded governesses for typically forty-hour work weeks, Nanny Pop-Ins grossed $50,000. By 1982 the company was making $150,000.

Employing over three hundred nannies, many of whom are degree-holding experts in child care, Nanny Pop-Ins strives to create the same happy, protective environment for children that Walt Disney's Mary Poppins did. Many of the company's nannies are with their charges around the clock, shopping for their clothes, teaching them lessons, doing their laundry, and preparing their meals. Some are nannies by day and graduate students by night. Others are grandmothers who haven't held a baby in years and miss the experience. Most are between the ages of 28 and 48.

One of the most memorable nannies Barbara Adamek ever employed taught a precocious girl of 2 how to play simple piano tunes and write stories. Like many other nannies, she's since gone on to her own field of specialization: teaching the handicapped. Since jobs for these experts are often few and far between, Adamek says many of them relish the opportunity of one-on-one tutoring in the meantime. You just can't get that experience working at a day care center. But her company's chief asset, she says, is "flexibility." Whatever a parent's specific requirements, Nanny Pop-Ins endeavors to satisfy them. Forty-hour work weeks are the norm, but those with variable schedules, such as flight attendants, can get nannies whenever they need them.

Feeling very successful today as she takes in around thirty to fifty phone calls a week, Adamek now consults nationally with other would-be entrepreneurs — through her new company, NPI Services, Inc. — to teach them how to start their own nanny companies. To date, several independent nanny companies have begun after utilizing NPI's consulting seminars. Among them: Nan-Ez of Tallahassee, Florida; Contemporary Nannies in Newport Beach, California; Nannies of Nashville, Nashville, Tennessee; Nanny's Here of Greensboro, North Carolina; and Neighborhood Nannies of Reston, Virginia. With the continuing nanny shortage, to meet the needs of a growing number of mothers who are entering the work force, Adamek expects NPI Services, Inc., to continue growing while bigger companies like KinderCare, a day care firm, have given up on the in-home child care services field. Experts like Beverly Benjamin of the American Council of Nanny Schools, Adamek points out, say that nanny demand outstrips nanny supply by one hundred to one. That kind of ratio is an entrepreneur's dream.

Frustrated in her search for an educational toy for her 1-year-old daughter, Lane Nemeth decided to start her own toy company. Today, Discovery Toys, a California-based company, is one of the great entrepreneurial success stories, grossing $40 million a year. Selling toys, games, and books the way some sell Tupperware or cosmetics, this direct selling business is one of the ten fastest-growing industries of the 1980s. But unlike Tupperware parties, which try "to get everyone warm and friendly with each other," Nemeth says, Discovery Toys parties involve some serious playing. "It's the only way parents can find out what's right for their child." Each of the company's salespeople — very few are men — is actually trained in child development so she can pinpoint the toy that fits each child's need.

The need is great for toy experts to come into the home and teach parents how to choose the games they can play with their children, Nemeth says. "If you're a typical adult shopping in a Toys 'R' Us, for example, you're likely to choose Monopoly or Clue or something you liked when you were a kid. You can't open the box and examine the contents, so you just buy what you know is good. Or you buy what the child absolutely has to have because they've seen it blitzed at them on Saturday morning television for three thousand months." On the other hand, a game like Enchanted Forest, one of her company's games, would probably remain on the store shelf, if sold at retail, even if it's the one your child would have liked best. Nemeth knew a lot about toys before she started her company, having bought thousands as the director of a day care center for disadvantaged children. She quit that job to start Discovery Toys in part because of the bureaucratic rules that hampered the state-run system.

"I didn't start this thinking, 'Oh, goody, I can be an international conglomerate.' I didn't know the first thing about business. I started it because I couldn't stand dealing with the state of California anymore. I said there's got to be another way to service parents and maybe I can make some money while I'm doing it." While still at the day care center, she remembers spending half her time "filling out stupid, idiotic forms that were meaningless — in quadruplicate, of course. In addition, every May, government officials would say, 'Oh, we've underspent our budget. Here's $10,000. Go out and spend it in thirty days, but . . .' It was a big 'but.' " The rules told her she couldn't spend the money on a much-needed van to take the children on field trips, even though some of them had never been to a supermarket, let alone anywhere else. No matter how full the toy boxes got, she had to buy more toys. It wasn't long before she became a toy expert.

So in 1977, armed with a B.A. in English literature, Nemeth risked her home and everything she had to borrow $50,000 and set up business in her garage. Despite her husband's temporary unemployment — he now has a seat on the Pacific Stock Exchange — she never stopped to worry about the future. "That's the way entrepreneurs succeed," she says. "They don't let any fears deter them. People always tell me that you have to risk. I don't buy that, because I think an entrepreneur doesn't see risk as risk. I don't think we define it the same way most people do." When friends told her she was crazy, she ignored them. "Maybe this is typical of entrepreneurs," she says. "You don't get influenced by outside sources. You're influenced by internal motivations."

Despite some initial success, the company almost went down the tubes in 1980. Unable to meet her payroll, and unable to obtain a reasonable loan to tide her over, Nemeth was forced to borrow money at a 27.5 percent interest rate. When things began to look their worst, however, she received a phone call from a venture capital firm that expressed an interest in investing in her company. As fate would have it, the wife of one of the investment firm's partners had been to a Discovery Toys demonstration party. She went home and told her husband, "This is a hot new company that with the right backing can go places."

"So they gave us money," Nemeth says, "and introduced us to a bank, and we've never been in that much trouble since. I sometimes think that our company is surrounded by an aura of good luck. And I'd like to think that it's because our mission is to help make children better." Part of her mission in life involves not neglecting her own child, Tara, whom she takes with her to conventions and who she hopes will become Discovery's chief executive officer someday. Their favorite nighttime activity is playing new games some of her company's 150-member staff design, like X from Outer Space.

Nemeth says that if she had been born twenty years earlier, when the role of women was looked at more narrowly than today, "I wouldn't have ever done what I'm doing now. It wouldn't have occurred to me that I was allowed." Moreover, before she got into business for herself, she admits, she had little appreciation of what was occurring in the business sector in terms of its job-creating potential for the nation's economy. Now as a successful businesswoman, she has become an evangelist for economic growth, believing that "without business and business entrepreneurs there'd be nothing." The biggest obstacle to business expansion, she thinks, is taxes. It doesn't seem fair, she says, that young, successful entrepreneurs face a huge increase in their taxes when they pass the $100,000 point. "They're still in the takeoff stage, and higher taxes can force them out of business."

The secret of her company's success? She considers each and every one of the Discovery Toys' sales force an entrepreneur, since each is responsible for her own success. More than 12,000 saleswomen (Nemeth prefers to call them "educational consultants") are selling her line of toys in every state in the Union as well as in Puerto Rico, Great Britain, and Guam. A few women who work especially hard at selling make upwards of $150,000 a year. But money is not the heart and soul of her business, she insists. It is children. "Even if a parent doesn't leave a Discovery Toys party with one of our products, they still go away with a much wiser eye and a new appreciation for the parenting role. When they buy their next toy and sit down to play with it with their children, they still might ask themselves if they really have the time to do it. But what else do we have in this world?'' she asks. ''With a good toy and new knowledge of how to use it, parents are more likely to find the time to spend with their children. And that's what this company is really all about.''

A rising tide lifts all boats.
— *President John F. Kennedy*

CHAPTER II

Agenda for Growth

IF WE HAVE LEARNED ANYTHING in the last half decade, it is that tax reduction and government deregulation, as far as they have gone, have paid handsome dividends in terms of expanding our economy, reducing inflation, lowering interest rates, stimulating new business formation, and creating a record-shattering number of new jobs.

We all remember the deafening cries of critics of deregulation, who warned that all manner of terrible things would befall this country — from higher inflation to widespread unemployment. Yet the remarkable result has been lower rates of inflation as a result of increased competition brought on by a spurt of entrepreneurial growth that has raised family incomes and produced more jobs. The number of new business starts in deregulated sectors of the economy has increased twice as fast as overall business starts nationally. One-fourth of the 20 million new jobs that were created between 1976 and 1982 were in deregulated industries, including trucking and telecommunications, banking and other financial services, and air travel.

Over the past decade or so, it is amazing how many times the opponents of deregulation have warned of economic disasters, and each time they have been proven wrong. For example, critics warned that if the oil and gas industries were deregulated, there would be skyrocketing oil prices and renewed gasoline shortages. The result has been just the opposite, with prices declining and an increased supply of oil and gas. The disintegration of the OPEC (Organization of Petroleum Exporting Countries) cartel has had much to do with this, of course, but our own efforts to deregulate our domestic energy industry have been an important factor as well. The deregulation of the airline industry begun in 1978, critics feared, would lead to sharp fare increases, fewer routes being offered, and reduced services. Yet, by 1986, there were at least seventy more airlines providing national, regional, and statewide services around the country than had been operating before deregulation began. Moreover, airline fares generally were substantially lower on most routes thanks to discounts and supersaver fares, and by 1985 the airline industry was recording its best earnings record in years. Similarly, critics of deregulation ominously warned that deregulation of the trucking industry would knock many trucking companies out of business, reduce services to out-of-the-way communities, and lead to higher shipping costs. On the contrary, more trucking companies are operating today, with improved services and at more competitive rates. This has been good for the small trucking entrepreneur as well as for businesses and consumers. In the same way, partial deregulation of the banking industry has led to higher and more competitive interest rates on savings, a broader array of improved services for banking customers, interest-bearing checking accounts, new forms of creative financing to serve consumer needs, and even lower interest rates charged on some bank-issued credit cards.

There are many more examples of how modest steps toward government deregulation have helped to spur economic growth and have benefited consumers. But as I have attempted to show in preceding chapters, there are still numerous regulatory barriers that remain stubbornly in place, vestiges of a bygone era in which economists and politicians believed that broad sectors of the economy could be run from Washington by government bodies. Our economy is paying a terrible price for these regulations in terms of a rate of economic growth far lower than is possible.

The same is certainly true of the tax cuts enacted in 1981, cuts that critics warned would trigger skyrocketing inflation and a deteriorating economy and would sap the treasury of needed revenues. Yet the cuts produced an economic resurgence that led the nation out of the worst recession since the Great Depression, helped achieve the lowest inflation rates in nearly a decade, and stimulated new business starts and employment. Opponents of the tax cuts said they were tax cuts for the rich, but the numbers from the Internal Revenue Service show that tax revenues from the rich didn't decrease, they increased. According to IRS data for 1982, federal tax revenue from those making between $100,000 and $500,000 rose 6 percent; revenue from those earning $500,000 to $1 million went up by 39 percent; and the tax take from those with incomes of more than $1 million went up by 42 percent. True, tax revenues declined in lower income categories, but only by 1 percent from those making between $50,000 and $75,000 and only by 4 percent from those earning between $20,000 and $50,000. But overall the tax cuts, by spurring economic growth, have helped to swell federal tax revenues. In fiscal 1982 the recession-starved federal tax receipts were $618 billion, but by fiscal 1987 the Congressional Budget Office was projecting them to hit $853 billion.

Nevertheless, reducing the marginal rates across the board, as beneficial as that has been, still leaves the tax rates too high to achieve a growing, dynamic economy in which there is economic opportunity for all. When John F. Kennedy was pursuing the presidency largely on the issue of the economy's lackluster performance, his rapid-fire response to those who said things aren't so bad was always "I think we can do better." In short, while much progress has been made to move America toward a free market economy, there are still many steps that can be taken to open up greater economic opportunities for all.

What is needed now is an agenda for greater economic growth, a blueprint through which we can stimulate increased business expansion; nurture the accumulation of venture capital for the creation of new enterprises, new inventions, and new technology; expand America's trading markets abroad; and build a more prosperous economy. The following agenda of economic growth proposals is intended to achieve these goals. Though my proposals are in no way intended to be a comprehensive, economy-wide blueprint for growth, they are intended to offer a broad sampling of tax, monetary, and deregulatory reforms that will not only stimulate higher levels of economic growth but will also alleviate some of the most stubborn domestic problems of our day through market-oriented mechanisms and solutions.

• Reform our federal tax code by further broadening the tax base and lowering the rates to provide greater incentives for economic growth, work, savings, and investment. Such reforms should lower the top personal tax rate to 25 percent; further reduce the capital gains tax and eventually eliminate it; double the personal exemption for all families to $2,000 to remove the working poor from the federal tax rolls; cut the current tax rate on savings in half and gradually eliminate it; increase the contribution ceiling for Individual Retirement Accounts, allowing nonworking spouses to contribute an equal amount to their own IRAs; and cut the corporate income tax rates by one-half over the next ten years.

Finally, in an effort to spark more small business growth, we ought to exempt small businesses from most federal taxation, at least during the critical first few years when fledgling business enterprises are just getting on their feet. Under a plan first proposed by Arizona governor Bruce Babbitt, small businesses would pay no corporate taxes on the first $250,000 to $500,000 earned. He would also exempt investors in such new firms from capital gains taxes on the first sale of stocks, thus encouraging greater venture capital investment in new enterprises. Babbitt would make up the lost federal revenue by closing tax loopholes used by large, established, capital-intensive corporations.

• Cut federal spending to bring the cost of federal programs into balance with a growing and productive economy. By substantially reducing government spending, Washington would be leaving more of the nation's savings and investment capital resources in the economy, fostering greater entrepreneurial expansion and growth. Economists generally agree that reduced government borrowing would lead to lower long-term interest rates, which would encourage greater business investment. Lower interest rates would also help to reduce the value of the dollar on foreign exchange markets, and that would in turn help to lower U.S. trade deficits.

• Enact legislation that would designate 150 of the poorest urban and rural communities in America as enterprise zones. These zones would be eligible for special federal tax breaks, deregulation of wage and labor laws, and other incentives for businesses to expand and locate within such zones and hire unemployed workers who reside there. Such legislation should establish a schedule under which new zones are added to the list as the economies of old zones regain their health.

• We must reform monetary policy at the Federal Reserve Board in order to achieve lower interest rates and bring about stability in the purchasing power of the dollar, ending the wild economic ups and downs of the last fifteen years. One solution worth enacting is set forth in the proposed Balanced Monetary Policy and Price Stability Act sponsored by congressmen Jack Kemp of New York and Jim Courter of New Jersey. It would direct the Federal Reserve Board to maintain price stability according to an index of commodity prices drawn up by the Fed and the U.S. Treasury. "Under this price rule," explains Courter, "the roller coaster ride that prices, interest rates, and exchange rates have been on since the early 1970s would have been mitigated. When the index of commodity prices rises, this would be a signal for the Fed to tighten policy. When the index falls, policy would be loosened." Such a guideline would have halted the inflationary fall in the value of the dollar in the 1970s as well as the deflationary rise of the dollar and high interest rates in the early 1980s.

• Abolish the Interstate Commerce Commission, allowing trucking, railroad, and other ground transportation companies and entrepreneurs the freest possible latitude to enter any markets they choose without federal approval as well as to raise or lower fares and rates at will. (Federal safety requirements, of course, must be preserved.)

• Enact a summertime June through September Youth Opportunity Wage at $2.50 an hour for youths under the age of 20, with a year-round wage differential provision for employers who combine the lower minimum wage with comprehensive job-training programs for unemployed youths.

• Enact an Urban Homestead Act that would sell existing public housing units to poor and low-income tenants. This proposal, similar to one successfully implemented in Great Britain by the Thatcher government, would allow public housing tenants to buy their rental units for about one-fourth their market value with little or no money down. Ownership would be voluntary, and no tenants could be evicted for choosing to continue renting. In effect, such a program would substitute mortgage payments for rent payments in the belief that tenants who own their homes are more likely to maintain them and make their payments on time. And, indeed, studies have shown that the quality of life in tenant-managed housing is vastly different from government-run public housing. According to a study by the American Enterprise Institute, a Washington-based think tank, "The tenant group far exceeded the performance of the other groups." In fact, under tenant self-management, the property was kept in tip-top condition, rental income doubled, crime fell by 70 percent, and even welfare dependency decreased.

Since its creation in 1968, the U.S. Department of Housing and Urban Development has poured more than $150 billion into a wide range of failed public housing and community development programs — from model cities to new communities — with not a lot to show for it. By turning over public housing units to their tenants and giving poor and low-income families the pride of home ownership, we have an opportunity to restore and repair the slum-infested neighborhoods of America's worst ghettos and save taxpayers a bundle of money to boot.

• There is, at the same time, a severe national shortage of housing for poor and low-income people, especially in our urban areas — a problem that has in many localities been exacerbated, if not caused, by rent control laws. To deal quickly with this problem, we should enact new tax incentives and generous depreciation schedules for investors and housing developers who finance and build low-income housing units.

• In a joint effort between the housing industry and federal, state, and local governments, undertake comprehensive legislative reforms and government-wide regulatory changes that will help bring down the cost of middle-income housing to more affordable levels. This will require leadership at the federal level to make needed modifications in federal housing, banking, and labor laws and regulations that prevent the housing industry from offering less expensive homes. Among the needed changes at the federal, state, and local level: elimination or modification of excessive housing regulations and specifications to help bring down construction costs; modifications in tax laws to help builders offer better long-range financing of new homes at lower interest rates; and further banking deregulation to encourage greater savings and increased investment in moderate-priced home building.

• In 1984, in a controversial ruling, the U.S. Department of Labor repealed its forty-two-year-old ban on home knitting of winter outerwear such as ski hats and sweaters. Now it is time to abolish the department's remaining 1942 Fair Labor Standards Act prohibitions against homeworkers involved in the making of jewelry, women's apparel, handkerchiefs, gloves and mittens, buttons and buckles, and embroidery. The action is sure to produce outraged opposition from the AFL-CIO and some of its member unions who want to extend the ban to telecommunicating, in which people perform computer and word-processing work at home. But the elimination of these counterproductive homeworker rules would open up a broad range of cottage industries that would provide gainful employment or supplemental income to millions of Americans, most especially poor and low-income families, particularly minorities and abandoned or divorced mothers. Not only does homework give people the freedom to work flexible hours of their own choosing, it allows mothers to care for their preschool children at home and run a business at the same time.

• Reform the antitrust laws by, among other things, abolishing the Federal Trade Commission's dual authority with the Justice Department over antitrust investigation and enforcement; modifying the Clayton Act to require that restrictions on entry, not a company's size or industry concentration, are considered anticompetitive practices; repealing the automatic trebling of damages for antitrust violations and substituting the "rule of reason" in assessing damages for violations; treating labor organizations the same as businesses under the antitrust laws; and clarifying the Sherman

Act to spell out that competitive success is not considered a violation of the antitrust laws.

• Modify the Securities and Exchange Commission's laws to make it easier for new financial companies to enter the marketplace and offer investment advice and brokerage services to consumers; and repeal the SEC's authority over financial publications that offer financial information, analysis, and investment advice.

• Reform U.S. export laws and regulations wherever possible to facilitate the export of American goods and services; and repeal any federal restrictions on U.S. exports where there are no foreign policy considerations. Among some of the changes that should be made: (1) repeal the 1977 Corrupt Practices Act, whose regulations have hamstrung U.S. businesses overseas, inhibited our ability to win major contracts, and given our competitors, who are under no such restrictions, a major advantage — especially in the Third World; (2) permit U.S. pharmaceutical firms to sell products abroad that are not approved by the U.S. Food and Drug Administration for sale here, but are approved by other countries; (3) accelerate the reduction of agricultural price supports to make U.S. farm exports more competitive in world food markets; (4) permit the export of timber being cut on federal lands and eliminate government restrictions that forbid the selling of Alaskan oil to Japan (economist Murray Weidenbaum, former chairman of the President's Council of Economic Advisers, says these two provisions alone would cut the U.S. trade deficit by $20 billion); (5) deregulate the U.S. shipping industry where government-imposed regulations have sharply driven up shipping costs for U.S. exporters, and, more specifically, repeal the Cargo Preference Act, whose rules require that a large part of our exports be shipped on more expensive American ships; (6) review and modify U.S. tax laws to encourage greater investment to modernize our industrial plants and thus make their products more competitive overseas; (7) and, finally, dismantle the outmoded and bureaucracy-heavy U.S. Department of Commerce, replacing it with a smaller but streamlined Department of Trade. The department's primary mission should be to help U.S. business, especially small to mid-sized businesses, find new overseas markets for their goods and services by assisting them in cutting through red tape both here and abroad.

• Repeal the Davis-Bacon Act of 1931, which requires contractors on federally funded building projects to pay the "prevailing" wage in the area where the project is being constructed. This law, in effect, ends up requiring that higher union wage scales are paid for federal construction projects rather than the average construction wage. Not only does this law unnecessarily add an estimated $1 billion a year to government building costs, it works against many poor and unskilled nonunion workers who are denied entry-level experience and on-the-job training. In addition, according to a Heritage Foundation study, Davis-Bacon "restricts the proportion of apprentices and lower skilled workers who can work alongside journeymen — again reducing the employment opportunities for young people.

"The net effect of the Act," the study continues, "is to transfer resources from taxpayers, consumers, nonunion workers and the unemployed to unionized construction workers and union contractors. Thus, not only does Davis-Bacon lower total economic output by misallocating resources, it reduces employment opportunities and redirects income to those typically paid above average wages." The act should be repealed.

• Abolish the U.S. Postal Service's Private Express statutes, which preserve the agency's wasteful and inefficient monopoly over first-class and related categories of mail. By opening up the mail industry to the freest competition from the private sector, we would be opening up hundreds of thousands of new jobs — especially entry-level employment in our inner cities, which would help to sharply reduce America's hardcore unemployed.

• Mandate the Federal Trade Commission to bring antitrust suits against states and localities that levy unreasonable occupational licensing fees, which discourage entry into various occupations and businesses. In many major cities of our land, municipal governments charge outlandishly excessive taxicab licensing fees, which prevent independent cabdrivers from starting their own business. In New York City, to take only one example, it costs more than $600 to obtain a taxicab "medallion" needed to operate a cab in the city. While the Federal Trade Commission has undertaken some tentative legal actions to get such fees reduced in certain municipalities, excessive occupational licensing fees or certification procedures for cabdrivers, barbers, beauticians, and other occupations and professions are the rule in most localities.

• Undertake a government-wide transfer of marginal federal programs and activities that could be more efficiently and inexpensively performed by the private sector. Better known as "privatization" in Great Britain, where it has been effectively implemented by the Thatcher government, aggressive contracting out offers two big dividends. First, it allows the government to cut spending by turning over activities that can be, and in many cases should be, performed by the business sector, without abandoning needed services and programs. At the same time, contracting out opens up business markets that have been monopolized by government, creating new commercial enterprises and more jobs.

For example, one of the areas ripe for privatization is the U.S. Coast Guard. An investigation by the Citizens for a Sound Economy, an independent economic study group, says taxpayers could save $1.6 billion over three years by privatizing many of the Coast Guard's marine services for pleasure boaters and commercial shipping interests. The Grace Commission found that the typical non-emergency Coast Guard tow is twelve times more costly than towing services provided by private firms. "Both emergency and non-emergency search-and-rescue responsibilities could be substantially turned over to the private sector," the study says, "either to sophisticated volunteer organizations," which are used successfully in Great Britain and Western Europe, or to commercial companies. The U.S. Sea Rescue company of Clearwater, Florida, for instance, is one of many firms that offer rescue and towing services similar to those of the American Automobile Association.

Other areas in which contracting out would create thousands of new jobs for the economy: in-house printing activities of the Government Printing Office, cleaning and food services, and building security, as well as maintenance, landscaping, accounting, management, and some logistical support services for our military bases.

At the same time, government could encourage a multitude of

new commercial enterprises if it simply removed itself from certain markets entirely, as the administration seeks to do with the sale of Conrail, the government's rail freight business, to the private sector. Other agencies and programs that should be sold to the private sector include the National Corporation for Public Broadcasting; National Public Radio; Amtrak, the government's rail passenger corporation; the U.S. Weather Service; the Overseas Private Investment Corporation, which insures big U.S. corporations investing abroad; and the Federal Housing Administration, which buys and sells home mortgages.

• And, finally, enact major new tax breaks for businesses operating job-retraining programs, allowing them dollar-for-dollar tax deductions for the costs of such programs. This will not only encourage businesses to expand their existing job-training programs, it will stimulate other firms to initiate new job-training programs of their own, which will in turn provide the level of job retraining needed to keep pace with the disappearance of smokestack industry jobs and the emergence and growth of new high-tech businesses.

For too long we have let politicians get away with murder — telling us they want to encourage economic growth and create more jobs and bring prosperity to every corner of our land. Again and again we have sent our lawmakers back to Washington, endlessly promising us they will "do something" to bring to America a renaissance of economic expansion. Yet in the end, the same obstacles and impediments to achieving full employment without inflation remain in America's dusty law books, and a more vigorous rate of economic growth remains a frustratingly elusive goal.

For too long we have been content to let the politicians tell us over and over again that "poverty is the problem," when, as economist Thomas Sowell of Stanford University's Hoover Institution so correctly noted, government-created impediments and obstacles to creating wealth are the chief problem. As a Heritage Foundation study aptly observed, "The nation's income and wealth will grow primarily as a consequence of the private actions of individuals who understand their own interests and who are encouraged through openness in markets, to compete for the dollars of consumers."

The challenge for America is to set about pursuing a new agenda that will allow such growth to occur unimpeded by government — the kind of economic growth that has made the United States the beacon of hope and opportunity for more than two hundred years.

Since the latter 1970s, the world has been moving, slowly and irregularly, in what is usually called a conservative direction. It has been tending away from the idea of state control of the economy and state responsibility for everything.

— *Robert Wesson*
HOOVER INSTITUTION

Marx sits up in heaven, and he is very powerful. He sees what we are doing, and he doesn't like it.

— *Deng Xiaoping*
LEADER OF CHINA

CHAPTER 12

The Triumph of the Free Market

"IF PRESENT TRENDS continue, the world in the year 2000 will be more crowded, more polluted, less stable ecologically . . . the world's people will be poorer . . . life for most people on earth will be more precarious."

This dark prophecy of worldwide doom and disaster was the conclusion of the *Global 2000* report, a $1 million crystal ball study put together by bureaucrats in the U.S. State Department, the Council on Environmental Quality, and eleven other federal agencies in the final year of President Jimmy Carter's forty-eight months of "national malaise." Born out of a growth-is-bad mythology that believes population growth causes poverty, disease, unemployment, crime, hunger, and insoluble environmental problems, *Global 2000* became a sort of biblical forecast for many political leaders and economic thinkers and activists who preached the coming of an Age of Sacrifice and Limitations. We must be prepared to do with less, they argued, to divide up the nation's wealth in smaller portions, because the world's strategic resources were being rapidly exhausted.

Among the *Global 2000* report's gloomier predictions: that there would be widespread poverty and resource depletion by the year 2000; the the extinction of "perhaps as many as 20 percent of all species on earth was a likelihood"; that the earth's water and air would be more polluted; that the prices of nonfuel minerals would rise by 5 percent annually between now and the year 2000. What was needed to forestall this series of global disasters, the report concluded, was an integrated global strategy among the world's nations, presumably a strategy in which governments would impose sweeping economic and social regulations and planning. In an address in 1983 to the Global Tomorrow Coalition, Carter observed that since the release of *Global 2000*, "other nations have adopted the report as a basis for shaping their national policies." Indeed, the report was the basis of much of Carter's own domestic policies, which emphasized conservation over increased production, shared sacrifices over expanding our resources, "national malaise" over hope, opportunity, and optimism.

Global 2000 came to symbolize the incurably pessimistic, status quo philosophy of no growth and declining resources that dominated a large part of America's intellectual and political power centers in the 1970s. But other thinkers, viewing the future as one of limitless potential for growth and improvement in the human condition, saw *Global 2000* for what it was — a shortsighted, confused, almost neo-Orwellian vision of the world's future. Julian Simon, a professor of economics at the University of Maryland, called the report "fatally flawed in method, lacking in historical foundation, and misleading in its conclusions about global trends it purports to describe." The late Herman Kahn, the brilliant physicist and futurist, called it "globaloney," noting that if human beings really behaved and thought the way the authors of the report predicted they would, then using the static analysis contained in *Global 2000* a man facing an oncoming train would soon be dead, "if present trends continue."

The Malthusians have long been with us, of course, crying that the earth will someday run out of food, fuel, and other natural resources, that our fragile planet is being rapidly overcrowded with people, who are stripping the landscape bare. In 1798 Thomas Malthus warned in his *Essay on the Principle of Population* that "population, when unchecked, increases in a geometrical ratio. Subsistence increases only in an arithmetical ratio." Thus, Malthus believed, the world's population would exceed its food supplies, resulting in mass starvation. Malthus's inherently flawed static analysis failed, among other things, to foresee mankind's unique ability, through invention and technology, to meet peoples' needs for food and other necessities. Indeed, since Malthus made his prophecy of doom, not only has world food production risen geometrically, the real price of food has been dropping. Yet today, like those who warned Columbus he would fall off the edge of the world, Malthus's disciples persist in believing that mass starvation is just around the next decade. In his 1968 best-seller *The Population Bomb*, ecologist Paul Ehrlich declared, "The battle to feed all humanity is over. In the 1970s the world will undergo famines — hundreds of millions of people are going to starve to death," he predicted. It never happened. Still, studies like the *Global 2000* report and its predecessor, *The Limits to Growth*, an equally gloomy study put out by the Club of Rome, have fed the superstitions and economic prejudices of people who believe that as the population grows the economic pie must be cut into smaller slices; that people are largely consumers instead of creators and producers and innovators, or, as Julian Simon says, "the ultimate resource"; and that the earth's resources are dwindling, when in fact the world's supplies of resources have been growing. In short, "the good news," as author Ben J. Wattenberg said in a book on worldwide economic, social, political, and demographic trends, is that "the bad news is wrong."

Consider population growth, for example. The World Bank's 1984 Annual World Development Report predicted that the earth's population will climb to 10 billion people by the year 2050, triggering a host of insoluble social and environmental problems. But in 1983 economist Thomas Sowell did a little simple mathematics, figuring out that all of the earth's then–4.4 billion people could easily fit into the state of Texas, which has 262,134 square miles of land area — with all of them living in typical middle-class, one-story, single-family homes, four persons to a house, each with a front and a back yard. Since then, of course, the world's population has grown to about 5 billion people, so Sowell's theoretical construction would perhaps require a little spillover into Oklahoma. Nevertheless, this is a stunning statistic that puts the world's population into a more rational, less hysterical light. The point is that the world is not elbow-to-elbow with people. It only looks that way to the professional end-of-the-worlders because they see dense concentrations of people in the cities. But, Sowell notes, "When the population of the United States was half of what it is today, its cities were *more* crowded than now. When Irish, Italian, Jewish immigrants were packed five or ten to a room in the slums of New York, one could travel through a hundred miles of open countryside in America without seeing a living soul (and still can today)." The point is that people have always flocked to the cities, because that's where they have found the most economic opportunities for themselves and their families.

But what about the assertion that as world population grows, poverty is the inevitable result? World Bank president A. W. Clausen flatly asserted in 1984 that higher population automatically "means lower living standards for hundreds of millions of people." In truth, the degree of poverty in a country has nothing whatsoever to do with its population density or even its supply of resources. It does, however, have a lot to do with each country's economic system and how free it is. Japan, for example, is one of the most prosperous nations on earth, but it has many more people per square mile (822) than, say, India (582), which is one of the world's poorest countries. Similarly, Singapore has a population density of more than 10,000 people per square mile, while famine-ravaged Marxist Ethiopia has 61 people per square mile, roughly the same as the United States. Yet Singapore's per capita income is over thirty times that of Ethiopia. Communist Albania has a relatively sparse population density of 246 persons per square mile but is the poorest nation in Europe, with a per capita income of $830. On the other hand, tiny but prosperous Switzerland, which has a free market economy, has a much higher population density — 403 persons per square mile. Yet Switzerland's per capita income, $14,408, is one of the highest in the world. There are five times as many people per square mile on the island of Taiwan as there are in China, yet Taiwan far exceeds China in per capita income, life expectancy, food production, and many other areas. Obviously, a country's population density has nothing to do with its relative health and prosperity.

It is no coincidence that the world's most prosperous countries are those with the freest and least-regulated, least-taxed economies. Asian economies like those of Japan, Singapore, Hong Kong, Taiwan, and South Korea are classic examples of these. All of these political entities are densely populated and have few or no major natural resources; yet they have high rates of economic growth, low unemployment, and rising per capita incomes. Indeed, despite Singapore's extremely high population density, the country's economic growth has been so robust it actually suffers from a shortage of labor, importing workers to take jobs in construction and other industries. "Fly over Hong Kong — a place seemingly without prospects because of insoluble problems a few decades ago — and you will surely marvel at the astounding collection of modern high-rise apartments and office buildings," says Julian Simon in a paper entitled *Treating People as an Asset.* "Then drive around on its excellent and smooth-flowing highways for an hour or two, and you will realize that a very large concentration of human beings in a very small area does not prevent comfortable existence and exciting economic expansion, if the economic system gives individuals the freedom to exercise their talents and to take advantage of opportunities."

These and other high-growth countries have sparked such growth through low tax policies that encourage savings, work, and business expansion and modernization. Gross private savings in Japan, for example, is 21 percent of disposable income. This compares to a savings rate of less than 6 percent of disposable income in the United States. The Japanese are able to attain such rates of savings for a number of reasons, cultural factors being one of them, but unlike the situation in the United States, the Japanese have savings accounts that are largely tax-free, similar to unlimited Individual Retirement Accounts. Moreover, there is no capital gains tax in Japan. That enables this tiny country to accumulate a huge savings pool to invest in new enterprises, modernize and expand its plants, and compete more effectively in foreign trading markets.

But what about food production? Are all densely populated countries starving? Once again, tiny, densely populated, but well-fed Japan provides an answer; this country has little arable land but uses what it has extremely efficiently within a free market economy. Meanwhile, "overpopulated" India, a nation of nearly 1.3 million square miles inhabited by 750 million people, has an enormous fertile landmass. Yet throughout the 1950s and early 1960s India was plagued by food shortages and famines. Today, it no longer is. India solved its food problems in the mid-1960s, after a near famine, with capitalist, supply-side solutions that poor Marxist and socialist nations in Africa and elsewhere, like Uganda and Ethiopia, would do well to emulate. For one thing, agricultural income in India was made exempt from taxes. The result has been substantially increased food production and fairer prices paid to farmers. Malcolm S. Forbes, Jr., deputy editor in chief of *Forbes* magazine, observes that India can better feed 750 million people today "than it could 350 million people at the time of its independence." Since 1970 India has doubled its wheat production and is seeking to sell its surpluses abroad. Its rice production alone has risen by more than 30 percent.

As for the myth that much of the world is plummeting toward mass starvation because food supplies have not kept pace with population growth, nothing could be further from the truth. "Many of the countries that only a decade ago were thought incapable of feeding themselves are doing just that today," says Ward Sinclair, agriculture reporter for the *Washington Post*. "The entire world of agriculture is standing on the edge of an unprecedented production explosion."

By 1985 Japan, Taiwan, and the Philippines were all struggling to cope with major rice surpluses. Bangladesh, which suffered from severe famines in the early 1970s, has become self-sufficient in food grains, and African nations are experimenting with new varieties of seed in white corn, cassava, and rice that promise higher yields and new hope for the peoples of West Africa. In Latin America, poor countries like Guatemala are actually exporting surpluses of rice, corn, and sorghum. And countries like Brazil and Argentina have huge expanses of rich farmland still waiting to be tilled, as do Canada and Australia.

The world's food revolution is due to a number of factors, including new high-yield strains of grain seeds, hardier crops, and improved agricultural technology in many parts of the world. But another major factor has been an effort in a number of collectivized or highly regulated economies to implement new market-oriented incentives for increased production and the achievement of wealth. For it has been regulations and tax disincentives which have discouraged higher farm production in many of the poorer regions of the world. A United Nations study, for example, found that during the 1970s per capita food production rose in every region of the world except one — the continent of Africa, whose largely state-controlled economies were among the most heavily regulated and taxed in the world. Zimbabwe (formerly Rhodesia) was once an agricultural exporting nation, but efforts by its Marxist government to collectivize once-prosperous farms have substantially cut agricultural production, forcing the country to import some of its food. In many cases, government price controls have had as much to do as anything else with poor agricultural production. "Most African countries actually discourage farm production by keeping food prices artificially low to placate city dwellers," writes reporter John Tierney in *Science 86* magazine.

The People's Republic of China, a nation with more than 1 billion mouths to feed, is perhaps the most breathtaking illustration of what can happen when even a little free market economics is inserted into a communist economy. Like India, China for decades couldn't provide enough food for its people. Food shortages and rationing were commonplace. The economy stagnated under the communal radicalism of Mao Tse-tung, which forbade any private ownership — even the keeping of goldfish. Then in the late 1970s and early 1980s, China, under the unorthodox leadership of Deng Xiaoping, began a series of sweeping economic reforms that, among other things, abolished the communes, leased land (which remains under state ownership) to family farmers, and allowed farmers to keep a portion of what they produced to sell in the marketplace for their own private gain. Moreover, leases were extended to from fifteen to thirty years and could be inherited; farmers could own farm animals and purchase their own machinery; merchants were allowed to establish shops. It wasn't long before these tightly controlled private markets began to flourish. Today, China is producing more food than it needs to feed its people. During the first half of the 1980s, China had achieved an astonishing 40 percent increase in food production. By 1985 it was expected to export 5 million tons of corn, roughly what Iowa produces. Among other farm commodities it is exporting is cotton, which it once imported at the rate of 4 million bales a year. China's economic reforms have been so successful, in fact, that it has since established farm export sales offices in Tokyo, among other major cities in Asia. China, says Dennis T. Avery, a senior agricultural analyst at the U.S. State Department, represents "one of the most dramatic and successful agricultural revolutions in world history."

Perhaps of even greater significance, China has gone so far as to establish special economic zones in several of its provinces, where a substantial degree of entrepreneurial profit-making and foreign investment enterprises are allowed to operate under the watchful eyes of the government. The purpose of this program is to see if controlled doses of capitalist investment can help develop an economic infrastructure in China that will lead to greater economic growth, more jobs, increased technological improvements, and higher incomes. It is perhaps one of the most incredible economic ironies in the world today that China's communist leaders dare to experiment with capitalism in enterprise zones in the hope of improving their economy, while in the land of capitalism Democratic leaders in Congress have refused to enact Ronald Reagan's enterprise zones proposal to bring economic growth and development to the poorest communities in the United States.

The point of all this is that the world is not headed into the economic abyss that *Global 2000* and other neo-Malthusians have forecast. On the contrary, there is substantial evidence that many of the world's most regulated economies are moving away from the paralyzing statism and collectivism that were so dominant throughout the 1960s and 1970s. "The dominant reality," says Robert Wesson, senior fellow at the Hoover Institution, "seems to be that efforts at economic planning have had a good trial and have turned out badly. Unable to manage effectively, leaders look to the marketplace to guide the economy."

This has been the path boldly pursued in Great Britain by the Thatcher government, which has been gradually "privatizing" England's still heavily nationalized economy — selling government-run businesses to the public and the commercial sector and opening up stagnant government monopolies to private sector competition. Since 1979 the British government has sold off a number of government-run companies — nationalized by a succession of Labor party governments — that were either losing money or operating inefficiently. Among them: British Petroleum (sold in October 1979), British Aerospace (sold in February 1981), National Freight Company (sold in February 1982), and British Telecom, the world's fourth largest telephone company (sold in November 1984). Not only did

Table 3
GREAT BRITAIN'S WORKING-CLASS REVOLUTION

The Thatcher Government's Sale of Nationalized Companies

Company	Date of Sale	Company Work Force Purchasing Stock (percent)
British Petroleum	October 1979	43
British Aerospace	February 1981	74
Cable & Wireless	October 1981	99
Amersham International	February 1982	99
National Freight Company	February 1982	36
Britoli	November 1982	72
Associated British Ports	February 1983	90
British Telecom	November 1984	96

Source: Madsen Pirie, "Buying Out of Socialism," *Reason* magazine, January 1986.

the government sell off badly run companies that were sapping the nation's tax resources, but it did it by selling shares in the companies to their own work force at special rates. Despite stiff opposition from organized labor officials, who generally opposed divestiture from the government, British workers jumped at the chance to become capitalists.

When British Telecom (BT), for example, went on sale in November 1984, "the reaction was frenzied," recalls Madsen Pirie, president of Britain's Adam Smith Institute, in *Reason* magazine. "Shares opened at 50 cents and rose to 97 cents within hours. At day's end, two million people had become stockholders, doubling in a single stroke the number of Britons who own stock. Overnight, British Telecom had become the nation's largest private company." Allen Partington, a warehouse worker, is a typical new stockholder. He told reporters for "American Interests," a PBS television program, "If I go to a bank and invest the money I intend to put with BT, I will get six percent, seven percent. It is not exciting. But when you can see it in the stock exchange and you can see it in the papers moving up or down, it gives you a little bit of excitement, you know, and I really enjoy that." Ninety-six percent of BT's workers purchased stock in their company.

Not only did Great Britain unload operations that were sapping the resources of its beleaguered taxpayers, and further weakening a deeply anemic economy, but in most instances, profitless, inefficient companies run by bureaucrats became moneymaking enterprises that in many cases showed sharply increased efficiency and productivity. Take the case of Jaguar, which the government-owned British-Leyland automobile company took over in 1966. Suffering from severe financial and management problems, poor quality, low productivity, and high worker absenteeism, Jaguar underwent an amazing turnaround after its sale in 1984, at which time 190 million shares were purchased by the public in a stock sale frenzy that caused traffic jams in London. The company's before-tax profits nearly doubled in just the first year of its operation as a privately owned business. New management and worker reforms were implemented, labor contracts were renegotiated, productivity rose, and pride of workmanship and quality returned. Similarly, since selling

Britain's nationalized trucking company, employee productivity at National Freight Company (NFC) has increased 30 percent. The company workers, notes Pirie, "have learned that private property and free markets are a good deal for everyone. Steven Shepherd, a driver with NFC who bought stock the first day it was offered, muses, 'You realize that part of this truck — it might only be very small now — is your money, you know, and it gives you that new edge.' "

In addition, the British government has sold off nearly 900,000 public housing units — representing 13 percent of Britain's public housing — to their low-income and middle-income tenants. Under this innovative program pushed through by the Thatcher government, public housing tenants were allowed to buy their homes at up to 50 percent below their market value, with the discount contingent upon how long they had lived in the unit. It has been hailed as "the largest single transfer of property since the dissolution of the monasteries by King Henry VIII in the 16th Century." Besides bringing in 5 billion pounds to the treasury, it sparked a dramatic change in what were deteriorating public housing properties as the new, proud owners worked hard at improving and maintaining their properties and making their payments on time. "To be honest with you, when you own a house you look after it more," one of the new owners told *American Interests* reporters. "You not only look after your own part, you also look after the surroundings as much as you can." Adds one resident cited by Pirie: "It's not difficult to determine which houses are privately owned. You can tell by alterations in front where people have done their doors — new doors, new windows, you know." Thatcher's privatization program in public housing is perhaps one of the most dramatic public welfare reforms in the history of Britain, or in any other country, for that matter. More important, it is working.

Significant economic changes are taking place elsewhere in the world as the Marxist and socialist examples have, one by one, shown themselves to be disastrous economic failures. China's mass mobilizations under Mao Tse-tung inflicted only more poverty on this vast country — suppressing perhaps the most entrepreneurial people in the world — while its free market Asian neighbors blossomed into economic dynamos. Meanwhile, the Soviet Union remains the ultimate example of a totally failed economy that must import massive amounts of agricultural commodities to feed its people. Since the 1970s, "the Soviet pace has slowed to a crawl or halted, and in some cases even gone backward," says the Hoover Institution's Robert Wesson. Its rate of economic growth has actually fallen back to about half of what it was in the 1960s. "Even life expectancy has sharply declined," says Wesson. "The Soviet Union is no longer a model of anything, except perhaps military organization. The effects of the discrediting of socialism in the Second Superpower have been profound."

Because the socialist, planned economic model has proven itself such a failure, I am convinced that before the decade of the 1980s is over many of the lesser developed nations of the earth will be turning increasingly toward economic growth initiatives to unleash the power of capitalism in their economies. Aside from China, nowhere is this dramatic turn of events more noticeable than in the preliminary but yet profound economic reforms being implemented in India by Prime Minister Rajiv Gandhi, who may be turning his country into the next economic miracle.

Many years ago Nobel Prize–winning economist Friedrich A. Hayek told *Forbes* magazine, "The best case of complete failure, thanks to too much planning, is India, where every mistake that could be made was made. I avoid going to India because I find it so uncongenial and depressing." Hayek would be delighted with what is happening in India today. Though the economic changes that have taken place there have received relatively little notice in the national news media, what Gandhi is doing to his economy could have far-reaching effects not only among his own people, but among Third World nations in Asia and throughout the world. Moving away from the socialist and trade protectionist policies pursued by his mother, Indira Gandhi, and his grandfather, Jawaharal Nehru, the young Gandhi staunchly believes that private initiative, entrepreneurial incentives, and increased foreign investment hold the key to leading his nation of 750 million people into a new era of economic growth and prosperity.

Indeed, in many ways Gandhi has become a practitioner and an exponent of Ronald Reagan's supply-side economics, boldly implementing some of its radical prescriptions for economic growth without entirely abandoning India's mixed economy, in which some capitalism is mixed with heavy government regulation. Under Gandhi personal income taxes have been slashed; estate taxes have been abolished; and counterproductive business licensing requirements and regulations, which were obstacles to new business expansion, have been sharply reduced.

Sounding like a supply-side disciple of Jack Kemp, Gandhi told a roundtable conference of industrialists from twenty-seven nations in New Delhi in April 1985 that India represented an enormous untapped market for consumer goods, especially electronic goods, and he invited the world's corporations to begin investing in India and taking advantage of its huge manpower pool. Such investment, he said, would help turn India into a "dynamic, self-reliant" economy. To encourage new investment in such core industries as agricultural technology, communications, and energy, Gandhi has even begun to remove regulations that have impeded foreign trade and investment, and he has lifted import duties on computers and other electronic equipment.

India still has a long way to go before it can even approach the dynamic models of other enterprising economies in Asia. But if India stays on its present deregulatory course, it could very likely become Asia's next success story. If it does, it will be largely due to Gandhi's open-mindedness and his ability to change and to adapt to a new era of enterprise in the world. Through their own wits and entrepreneurial spirit, much Western aid, and the rise of economic growth in the region generally, large numbers of Indians have lifted themselves out of poverty and into what Gandhi calls the takeoff stage. His bold vision: to open up India's vast market to a multitude of goods and services that, in turn, will create new businesses and jobs for his people.

Interestingly enough, Gandhi does not talk of competing with exporting nations like Taiwan and Japan, although that, too, may come one day. Rather, he emphasizes the need to encourage India's technological development and the growing purchasing power of India's consumers. "We can depend on our own market," Gandhi told the foreign industrialists, noting that when India temporarily lifted import restrictions on color television sets for the 1982 Asian Games, consumers in India bought out the available supply, proving the country's growing strength as a consuming nation.

However, there is much more riding on Rajiv Gandhi's latest free market initiatives than the economic future of the world's largest democracy. For if Gandhi's bold reforms succeed in India, they can succeed in the Third World nations of Africa, the Middle East, Southeast Asia, and Latin America. And if that begins to happen, as I believe it will, then the Soviet Union's disastrous socialist experiment will cease to be a model for the impoverished have-not nations of the world.

At the same time, it would be a grievous error to conclude from all this that the world is in some headlong rush toward a new era of aggressive capitalism, slashing taxes, abolishing regulations, and pruning government bureaucracies. The painful and crushing reality is that there are many countries and regions of the world that have yet to grasp the economic promise of growth and prosperity that awaits those who release their economies from the stranglehold of high taxes, excessively costly government programs, and insidious regulations.

There can be no sadder example of this in the Western world than on the continent of Europe, where once burgeoning economies are now stagnating under the double yoke of oppressive tax rates and smothering economic regulations. In the early 1960s, total tax revenues for the Western European nations, collectively part of the Organization for Economic Cooperation and Development (OECD), averaged 32 percent of Gross National Product — roughly the tax burden that one now finds in the United States (33 percent) and Japan (31 percent). Today, however, Europe's economies are being strangled in excessive taxation needed to support huge government bureaucracies and social welfare programs. A look at Table 4 shows how those tax burdens have climbed over a twenty-year period. In Sweden, for example, tax revenues consume nearly 60 percent of the total GNP; in the Netherlands, 56 percent; Norway, 53 percent; Denmark, 51 percent; France, 47 percent; and West Germany, 45 percent. By 1982, the last year for which figures are

Table 4
TOTAL TAX RECEIPTS OF GOVERNMENT AS A PERCENTAGE OF GNP

	1962	1972	1982
United States	27.0	30.0	32.0
Japan	21.6	21.5	30.2
West Germany	36.6	39.8	45.3
France	36.3	38.2	46.9
United Kingdom	33.1	36.8	43.7
Italy	29.1	30.9	41.5
Canada	27.0	35.9	39.0
Austria	34.0	41.1	46.7
Belgium	29.2	35.5	45.4
Denmark	28.2	45.9	50.7
Finland	30.1	36.3	39.7
Greece	23.2	26.6	—
Iceland	27.5	34.5	—
Luxembourg	33.5	38.2	—
Netherlands	34.4	48.0	55.8
Norway	35.5	48.4	52.7
Portugal	19.3	23.4	—
Spain	17.5	23.0	—
Sweden	35.5	49.9	59.6
Switzerland	23.9	26.4	33.2
OECD Europe	32.7	37.1	45.7

Source: Organization for Economic Cooperation and Development, *OECD Economic Outlook,* July 1984.

available, total tax receipts for the European OECD nations averaged 46 percent of GNP.

Table 5 shows the disastrous effects those high levels of taxation have had on the so-called free market European economies. "Whereas Europeans could brag about brisk economic growth during the 1960s and early 1970s," says William Orzechowski, director of economic policy for the U.S. Chamber of Commerce, "their countries now breed economic stagnation. Throughout most of the 1960s, when Europe's tax burden was relatively light, real economic growth averaged 4.5 percent. However, as the average tax burden of OECD Europe nudged toward the 40 percent mark in 1973, its real economic growth rate tumbled to a paltry 1.8 percent. By comparison, the relatively moderate tax countries — Japan and the U.S. — have

Table 5
AVERAGE PERCENTAGE GROWTH OF REAL GNP AT MARKET PRICES

	1964–74	1974–82	1983–84*
OECD Europe	4.5	1.8	1.7
Japan	8.8	4.3	4.9
United States	3.9	2.3	5.5

Source: Organization for Economic Cooperation and Development, *OECD Economic Outlook,* July 1984.
* Based on Data Resources, Inc., estimates.

experienced substantially higher growth over the past ten years, with the U.S. currently the leader among developed countries. However, in the 1970s, even the U.S. and Japan suffered a slowdown in growth as their tax burden rose.''

Europe's economic anemia has produced a crisis in job development. In 1985 the Organization for Economic Cooperation and Development midyear review of the economic outlook declared that unemployment in Europe ''is at its highest rate in more than 50 years.'' By the end of 1985, the OECD outlook report showed that the labor force in most of its member countries was growing faster than the number of available jobs. The biggest exception was the United States which had pushed total employment to a record 109 million jobs. Among OECD countries generally, however, there were over 31 million jobless in 1985, compared to 10.3 million in 1970. But, noted *The Economist,* the unemployment ''gloom is concentrated in Europe. Its unemployment is rising almost everywhere. . . .''

There is an incurable tendency among most of Europe's political and economic elite to blame the United States — from the U.S. deficit to the American dollar — for virtually all of its economic problems. But, observes economist Paul W. McCracken of the University of Michigan, ''European governments would do well to concentrate more of their energies on the homegrown aspects of their problems. Their economies do suffer from rigidities in the deployment of labor and other productive resources. Laws that limit the scope to eliminate redundant workers, quite generous unemployment compensation made almost indefinitely available, overly high minimum wages — these, taken in the name of welfare, are a powerful program for producing chronic unemployment. And these rigidities have made a major contribution to Europe's economic sclerosis. Responsibility for freeing up their economies, so that they can once again deliver enlarging job opportunities and rising real incomes, is squarely with governments there." Let Europe, for openers, begin questioning how its economy can possibly grow as long as government outlays as a percentage of GNP are running 50 percent or more. The European nations have strengthened their public sector with an explosion of public expenditures at the expense of their private sector, which has grown dangerously weak and undernourished.

The lesson of Europe's economic stagnation and America's resurgence should be clear to all who want to encourage greater economic growth throughout the world's developed and less-developed nations. It is simply this: excessive levels of taxation and government regulation of the marketplace and economic decision making will weaken the foundation of work, savings, investment, and competition upon which a healthy and vigorous economy rests. "The time has come for Europe to have done with liturgical preoccupations and once again find the route to activating the forces of vigorous economic progress," McCracken correctly suggests. But is this a lesson that Europe and the other economically weak nations of the world will learn in time?

My belief is that they will, as long as there are successful economic models from which nations can judge their own experiences and compare sharply contrasting economic performances. As depressing as the collective performances of the European nations have been, not to mention the similarly overregulated less-developed nations that have taxed their economies to their knees, there still is much reason to feel bullish about the future. And the reason is that clearly more and more countries are turning to capitalist, market-oriented solutions to solve their fiscal and economic problems rather than to government solutions — both in the free world and some communist countries as well.

With China slowly experimenting with increasing doses of capitalism; with India cutting its personal tax rates, eliminating some of its socialist and protectionist-inspired regulations; with Great Britain making significant strides to privatize its nationalized economy and reawaken its entrepreneurial spirit; and with so many thriving economic free market models emerging in Asia and elsewhere, capitalism is suddenly in the ascendency in the 1980s. Even some of the Soviet bloc nations of Eastern Europe, such as Yugoslavia, Hungary, and Romania, have moved slowly but deliberately away from collectivization and toward greater degrees of entrepreneurial freedom. The United States can help encourage this economic movement by further freeing its own economy from regulatory obstacles, burdensome government, and excessive, counterproductive tax rates and becoming an irresistible role model for the nations of the world.

This is why America's chief social and political challenge for the remainder of this decade must be to seek out and destroy government-created obstacles and disincentives to greater economic growth; to initiate creative new incentives that will encourage greater levels of enterprise and individual achievement in every corner of our land; and, most of all, to bring about full employment with low inflation for all our citizens. Meeting that challenge will not only keep and renew America's promise as the land of opportunity but light a beacon for all the nations of the world to follow toward a brighter and more prosperous future.

Index